STUDY GUIDE TO BIBLICAL ELDERSHIP

TWELVE LESSONS FOR MENTORING
MEN FOR ELDERSHIP

ALEXANDER STRAUCH

LEWIS & ROTH PUBLISHERS
PO BOX 569 • LITTLETON, COLORADO 80160 USA
www.lewisandroth.org

All Scripture quotations, except those noted otherwise, are from the *New American Standard Bible,*
Copyright © 1960, 1962, 1963, 1968, 1972, 1973, 1975, 1977, 1988, 1995
The Lockman Foundation. Used by permission.

Quotation by Neil T. Anderson is taken from *The Bondage Breaker* by Neil T. Anderson.
Copyright © 1990 by Harvest House Publishers, Eugene, Oregon. Used by permission.

Discover Your Gifts is published by CRC Publications, Copyright © 1989,
2850 Kalamazoo Ave. SE, Grand Rapids, MI. Used by permission.

ISBN 0-936083-13-1

Cover Design: Stephen T. Eames

Editors: Stephen and Amanda Sorenson

Printed in the United States of America

08 07 06 05 04 03   13 12 11 10 9

TO RECEIVE A FREE CATALOG OF OTHER BOOKS PUBLISHED BY
LEWIS AND ROTH PUBLISHERS, CALL TOLL FREE: 1-800-477-3239
(303-794-3239 LOCAL/INTERNATIONAL) Fax: 303-794-3116

Contents

LESSON 1

OLD TESTAMENT ELDERS - JOB

Lesson 1 explores Job's life as a model of the Old Testament elder. We will examine the duties and deficiencies of Israel's elders and will note the failure of Job's colleagues to compassionately and tactfully minister to him during his intense suffering. This lesson will help you think and act like a biblical, Christlike elder. The lesson covers pages 121-124, 186-202, 227-238.

LESSON 2

MEN OF SOUND DOCTRINE AND WISDOM - ACTS 15:1-35; 21:18-25

Lesson 2 sets forth the biblical imperative that elders know Bible doctrine so that they will be adequately equipped to judge doctrinal ´disputes and provide wise, godly counsel and leadership for the congregation. As you will discover throughout the *Guide*, biblical elders must be men of the Word. The biblical standard for pastor elders is that they be able to teach and defend sound Christian doctrine. Elders who are biblically inadequate are actually a curse to the church, not the blessing God would have them be. This lesson is intended to help you evaluate your preparedness as a teacher and defender of Christ's doctrine. It will also touch briefly on the elder-congregation relationship and the need for elders to be men of wisdom who know how to lead the congregation in godly decision making. The pages to be read are 17-22, 125-133, 291-295.

LESSON 3

THE FIRST ELDER APPOINTMENTS - ACTS 14:23
"GUARD YOURSELVES" - ACTS 20:28*a*

In this lesson we will be confronted by the significance of Acts 14:23 to the New Testament doctrine of eldership and learn to think accurately about the Greek word for "appointed," which is frequently misinterpreted to mean church election or ordination.

Most of the lesson covers Acts 20:28a: "Be on guard for yourselves." Shepherds cannot guard others from Satan's many deceptions if they do not first guard their own souls. This lesson reinforces the Lord's call for us to be men of the Word and of prayer. The pages to be read are 133-147.

LESSON 4

PROTECTING THE FLOCK FROM FALSE TEACHERS - ACTS 20:18-35
THE SOURCE OF THE ELDERS' STRENGTH - ACTS 20:32, 36-38
THE PAULINE MODEL FOR ELDERS - ACTS 20:33-35

Lesson 4 deals with the elders' solemn duty to protect their flock from "savage wolves," that is, false teachers. It covers Paul's farewell message to the Ephesian elders in Acts 20:18-35. An elder who desires to be a faithful guardian of Christ's Word and flock must become thoroughly familiar with this Scripture passage. It answers the question of who places elders in the local church as overseers and pastor shepherds, and establishes the inestimable worth of the body of Christ, which elders are called to guard from Satanic workers.

The second half of the lesson addresses the elders' need to trust in God and His Word for strength and guidance. It also explores Paul's example of self-employment and generosity to others. The reading covers pages 17-22, 27-29, 31-34, 109-115, 140-159.

LESSON 5

HUMBLE SERVANTS AND THE CHIEF SHEPHERD - 1 PETER 5:3b-5
HARD-WORKING MEN - 1 THESSALONIANS 5:12, 13

Lesson 5 covers 1 Peter 5:1a, 3b-5 and 1 Thessalonians 5:12, 13. Peter exhorts elders to shepherd the flock through the power of personal example and encourages them with the promises of the glorious return of the "Chief Shepherd" and the "crown of glory." Finally, he calls elders, as well as the flock, to clothe themselves with humility so that all may live together in peace.

Paul's exhortation to the congregation at Thessalonica reinforces the elders' task of leading and admonishing the congregation. In order to bear this great responsibility, pastor elders must be self-disciplined, highly committed disciples of the Master. Clearly, board elders cannot pastor a local church: only hard-working, self-disciplined, shepherd elders can.

Like Peter, Paul also calls the congregation and its leaders to work for peace and to love one another. Without humility, love, and peace there is little hope of experiencing the joys of Christlike community and effective pastoral leadership. The pages to be read are 161-174, 249-252.

LESSON 6

TEAM LEADERSHIP - PHILIPPIANS 1:1, 1 TIMOTHY 5:17, 18

Lesson 6 examines the plurality of overseers mentioned in Philippians 1:1, the equating of overseers with elders, the significance of church leadership terminology, the importance and practice of team leadership, and the principle of "first among equals."

The major focus of the lesson is on learning how to work with fellow elders in Christian harmony, which is not an easy task. Becoming a good team player takes years of effort and commitment. The key to team leadership is *agapē* love. The lesson covers pages 31-50, 101-117, 174-180.

LESSON 7

QUALIFIED LEADERS - 1 TIMOTHY 3:1-15

The major emphasis of lesson 7 is the necessity of church elders being "above reproach." The lesson also reviews Paul's purpose in writing 1 Timothy, the Ephesian elders' failure to protect the church from false teaching, the faithful saying of 1 Timothy 3:1, and the qualifications for overseers. The pages to be read are 67-83, 181-202.

LESSON 8

HONORING AND DISCIPLINING ELDERS - 1 TIMOTHY 5:17-25

Lesson 8 surveys 1 Timothy 5:17-25, one of the most significant New Testament passages on the doctrine of Christian eldership. It focuses on elders who deserve double honor because of their capable leadership and diligent labor in the Word and explains the necessity of evaluating each elder's gifts.

The passage also addresses the difficult issue of disciplining elders who have been proved guilty of sin. The lesson emphasizes the need for leaders to be courageous in exposing sin, to judge justly, and to follow the New Testament precautions in appointing elders. The pages to be read are 206-224.

LESSON 9

APPOINT ONLY QUALIFIED MEN - TITUS 1:5-11

Lesson 9 reviews Paul's instructions to Titus and the underdeveloped churches on the Island of Crete that were facing attack from false teachers. Paul sets forth the qualifications for elders: church elders must control personal anger, be hospitable, be faithful to Christian doctrine, and be able to exhort in sound doctrine and refute false teachers. The lesson also examines the terms "ordination" and "appointment," and the unbiblical division between clergy and laity. The lesson covers pages 104-106, 111-114, 202-205, 225-238, 284-288.

LESSON 10

SHEPHERD GOD'S FLOCK IN GOD'S WAY - 1 PETER 5:1-3

In lesson 10, Peter's farewell exhortations to the elders of northwestern Asia Minor in 1 Peter 5:1-3 are considered. We examine the urgent apostolic imperative for elders to shepherd God's flock, that is, to be all that shepherds should be to the flock. This lesson will help you think practically about your time commitment to the shepherding task and your personal contribution to the shepherding team.

Furthermore, this passage is an urgent call for pastor elders to shepherd the flock in a distinctly Christlike way–willingly, eagerly, and as godly models of Christ–not as authoritarian tyrants or hirelings. Christian elders are to be loving, servant leaders. The lesson requires that you read chapter 5, "Servant Leadership," in *Biblical Eldership*. It covers pages 9-31, 85-98, 114, 149, 239-248.

LESSON 11

CARING FOR THE POOR - ACTS 11:29, 30; 20:35
PRAYING FOR THE SICK - JAMES 5:13-16

Lesson 11 addresses the elders' attitude toward the poor and needy, and the character qualities necessary in the men who administer the church's charitable funds. The second half of the lesson deals with the elders' responsibility to the sick, as described in James 5:14, 15. To be a Christlike shepherd, the elder must be compassionate toward those who suffer. In ministering to the sick, the pastor elder must be a man of faith, prayer, and wise counsel. The pages to be read are 29-31, 156-159, 253-263; also referenced are pages 188-202, 228-238.

LESSON 12

SPIRITUAL WATCHMEN - HEBREWS 13:17
SUBMISSION TO AUTHORITY - HEBREWS 13:17
MALE LEADERSHIP - 1 TIMOTHY 2:9-3:2*a*

The final lesson explores Hebrews 13:17. We discuss the institutional church model versus the community church model, and the joys and heartaches of leading God's people. In addition, the subject of submission to church elders, a matter of great disdain to modern man, is studied.

We also study chapter 3 of *Biblical Eldership*, "Male Leadership." Of utmost importance to the Lord's people, this is not only an issue of God's plan for male-female relationships in the home and church, but one of biblical integrity and authority. The lesson covers pages 51-66, 265-273.

SCRIPTURE INDEX

GENERAL INDEX

FUTURE ASSIGNMENTS AND DISCUSSIONS

ACKNOWLEDGMENTS

Enthusiastic words of thanks are given to Dick and Anne Swartley who have spent untold hours meticulously pouring over each assignment and question and designing the *Study Guide to Biblical Eldership*. Without them the *Study Guide* would not be the valuable tool it is today. Their work has been a labor of love on behalf of God's people.

Thanks are also due to Todd Leopold for his critique of each lesson as a mentoree; to John Ellis for his analysis of each lesson as an experienced shepherd elder; to the elders of the First Evangelical Free Church in Lakeland, Florida who worked through the *Study Guide* together, resulting in many helpful suggestions; and to Barbara Peek for proofreading the final copy.

AUTHOR

Alexander Strauch lives with his wife and four children in Littleton, Colorado. He is also the author of the *New Testament Deacon: The Church's Ministry of Mercy* and *The Hospitality Commands*. Mr. Strauch has been a teacher and an elder at the Littleton Bible Chapel for the past twenty-five years.

ABBREVIATIONS

BOOKS OF THE BIBLE

Old Testament

Gen.	Genesis	Ezra	Ezra	Dan.	Daniel
Ex.	Exodus	Neh.	Nehemiah	Hos.	Hosea
Lev.	Leviticus	Est.	Esther	Joel	Joel
Num.	Numbers	Job	Job	Amos	Amos
Deut.	Deuteronomy	Ps.	Psalms	Obad.	Obadiah
Josh.	Joshua	Prov.	Proverbs	Jonah	Jonah
Judg.	Judges	Eccl.	Ecclesiastes	Mic.	Micah
Ruth	Ruth	Song	Song of Solomon	Nah.	Nahum
1 Sam.	1 Samuel	Isa.	Isaiah	Hab.	Habakkuk
2 Sam.	2 Samuel	Jer.	Jeremiah	Zeph.	Zephaniah
1 Kings	1 Kings	Lam.	Lamentations	Hag.	Haggai
2 Kings	2 Kings	Ezek.	Ezekiel	Zech.	Zechariah
1 Chron.	2 Chronicles			Mal.	Malachi
2 Chron.	2 Chronicles				

New Testament

Matt.	Matthew	Phil.	Philippians	James	James
Mark	Mark	Col.	Colossians	1 Peter	1 Peter
Luke	Luke	1 Thess.	1 Thessalonians	2 Peter	2 Peter
John	John	2 Thess.	2 Thessalonians	1 John	1 John
Acts	Acts of the Apostles	1 Tim.	1 Timothy	2 John	2 John
Rom.	Romans	2 Tim.	2 Timothy	3 John	3 John
1 Cor.	1 Corinthians	Titus	Titus	Jude	Jude
2 Cor.	2 Corinthians	Philem.	Philemon	Rev.	The Revelation to
Gal.	Galatians	Heb.	Hebrews		John (Apocalypse)
Eph.	Ephesians				

HOW TO USE THE *STUDY GUIDE TO BIBLICAL ELDERSHIP*

Friends of ours who are elders in another church were discussing the need to train more men for eldership. As they sought suitable material for training potential elders, one reminded the others that, "No one ever trained us!" Unfortunately, this assessment could be echoed by 95 percent of all elders and deacons.

WHY SHOULD MEN BE TRAINED FOR ELDERSHIP?

The lack of elder and deacon training is an extremely critical problem. We are not training the very men who lead and have oversight of our churches. We erroneously believe that our serving elders and deacons understand spiritual oversight and care, but in fact our churches are filled with elders and deacons who confess that they are unprepared and untrained for their work. Even Bible schools and seminaries, for the most part, do not prepare men to provide spiritual care or leadership for a congregation.

This lack of training is not uncommon among organizations that operate in a familial manner. A leading news magazine reported on the amazing strength of America's family-owned businesses, estimating that "nearly 50 percent of the nation's gross national product" was produced by family-owned firms.[1] After enumerating many positive aspects of the family-owned business, however, the article reported that its chief weakness is its failure to train the next generation of family leaders: "On the whole, only a third of family-owned companies survive into the second generation because founders often are too busy to plan ahead or because they lack confidence in their young."[2]

The local church is an extended family that does God's business. Like many family-owned businesses, local churches fail to train the next generation of leaders. Church leaders are frequently too preoccupied with the work of the church or lack vision for training future leaders. They have seriously underestimated both the need and their responsibility. Like flowers in spring, leaders who are ready to bless the flock will not appear without planting or preparation.

Kenneth O. Gangel, a biblically sound expert in church management and training, is right on target when he points out, "The key to reproducing leadership is to clearly plan for it."[3] "Church leaders," exhorts Gangel, "need to produce leaders who will reproduce leaders precisely as it is done in the family–through experience, instruction, and modeling."[4]

Training men for future leadership and ministry should not be a novel concept to the Christian who is familiar with what the Bible teaches. Our Lord and Savior Jesus Christ spent a significant part of His public ministry preparing for the future. He patiently poured His life into twelve men, training them to be the future leaders of the church. He was a master teacher and mentor. Scottish biblical professor and writer, A. B. Bruce (1831-1899), in his standard-setting work, *The Training of the Twelve*, writes:

"Follow Me," said Jesus to the fishermen of Bethsaida, "and I will make you fishers of men." These words . . . show that the great Founder of the faith desired not only to have disciples, but to have about Him men whom he might train to make disciples of others. . . . Both from His words and from His actions we can see that He attached supreme importance to that part of His work which consisted in training the twelve. In the intercessory prayer [John 17:6], e.g., He speaks of the training He had given these men as if it had been the principal part of His own earthly ministry. And such, in one sense, it really was. The careful, painstaking education of the disciples secured that the Teacher's influence on the world should be permanent; that His kingdom should be founded on the rock of deep and indestructible convictions in the minds of the few, not on the shifting sands of superficial evanescent impressions on the minds of the many.[5]

Like his Lord, Paul was also a discipler of men. He had his Timothys, and he expected his Timothys to train others: "The things which you have heard from me in the presence of many witnesses, entrust these to faithful men who will be able to teach others also" (2 Tim. 2:2). Paul expected that when Timothy departed from Ephesus he would leave in place trained, faithful men who would continue the development of future teachers and leaders.

It should not be assumed that men trained in a seminary are exempt from the need for specialized preparation for the responsibilities of being a pastor elder. Unfortunately, seminaries train a man to be the leader of "his own" congregation rather than an equal participant on an elder council. Seminary graduates who receive significant preparation in the application of scriptural principles to the governance and care of the church are a blessed exception to the rule.

Elder training is essential to the church's response to the great commission. Our Lord's command to go, to teach, and to make disciples of all the nations–in other words, the discipleship process–cannot be sustained without elders. In any mission field, whether it be local or at a great distance culturally, the planting of new churches is paced by the availability of elders. The stability of those new churches and their ability to grow will be determined by the maturity of their founding elders.

THE TERM "PASTOR ELDER"

Throughout the *Study Guide*, as in *Biblical Eldership,* elders are referred to as "shepherd elders" or "pastor elders." This is to counter the considerable amount of unscriptural thinking about elders that exists today. When most Christians hear of church elders, they think of lay church officials, committeemen, executives, policymakers, or advisors to the pastor. They do not expect church elders to teach the Word or be involved pastorally in the lives of people. We refer to such elders as "board elders." They are not true biblical elders.

The contemporary, church-board concept of eldership is irreconcilably at odds with the New Testament's definition of eldership. According to the New Testament concept, elders lead the church, teach and preach the Word, protect the church from false teachers, exhort and admonish the saints in sound doctrine, visit the sick and pray, and judge doctrinal issues. To use biblical terminology, elders shepherd, oversee, lead, and care for the local church. Therefore, to communicate accurately the New Testament concept of eldership, it is necessary to explain that the New Testament term *elder* means "pastor elder," "shepherd elder," or "pastor." Throughout the *Study Guide*, we use these terms interchangeably to distinguish between "board elder," the unscriptural concept, and "shepherd elder," the biblical concept. For further explanation of the differences, read pp. 15-17, 31-34 in *Biblical Eldership*.

ELDER QUALIFICATIONS

Since the New Testament so emphatically emphasizes the moral and spiritual qualifications of elders, we underscore them throughout this *Guide*. Most elder leadership problems can be traced directly to the failure on the part of an elder or the body of elders to act according to a specific New Testament character qualification. As there is such a profound depth of wisdom contained in each Spirit-given qualification, elders need to be thoroughly familiar with each. If you need help defining the New Testament elder qualifications, read pp. 188-202 and 228-238, in *Biblical Eldership*. See p. 15 of this introduction for a complete list.

USING THE *STUDY GUIDE*

The *Study Guide to Biblical Eldership: Twelve Lessons for Mentoring Men for Eldership* is designed primarily as a study tool for training prospective new elders. It consists of twelve lessons based on the revised and expanded edition of Alexander Strauch's *Biblical Eldership: An Urgent Call to Restore Biblical Church Leadership* (1995). The *Study Guide to Biblical Eldership* is to be used by the prospective new elder (the mentoree or trainee) under the direction of a mentoring elder. The prospective elder reads *Biblical Eldership* (the revised edition of 1995) and works through the lessons in the *Study Guide to Biblical Eldership*. After completing each lesson, he meets with his mentoring elder to discuss the questions and assignments. A companion volume, *The Mentor's Guide to Biblical Eldership,* by Alexander Strauch and Richard Swartley, is available to assist the mentoring elder.

If your church does not have a training program for prospective elders, you may seek out one of your church's elders and ask him to participate in this study program by serving as your mentor. Although the *Study Guide* was prepared to be used in a mentoring relationship, if no elder in your church is available, an aspiring elder can use the *Study Guide* in a self-directed study.

BEFORE STARTING THE *STUDY GUIDE*

Scripture states most emphatically that a new convert cannot be an elder (1 Tim. 3:7) and that a man is not to be appointed an elder in a hasty manner (1 Tim. 5:22). Thus the *Study Guide* is designed for mature Christian men who are **already actively involved** in local church service, teaching, and leadership. It is for those who know the Scriptures, are knowledgeable in basic Bible doctrines, and agree with the doctrinal positions of the local church. It is for those who desire pastoral eldership (1 Tim. 3:1), and those whom the elders have selected for training for possible eldership. It is assumed that those who use the *Study Guide* are experienced in serving in the church and are well-known by the elders. Moreover, prospective elders should recognize that entering the mentoring process does not guarantee that they will be appointed elders at its conclusion.

Depending on the mentoree's experience, knowledge, skills, personal desire, and needs, the lessons can be accomplished in six months or spread out over a year or two. The lessons should be used in a flexible manner, depending on the mentoree's progress and interest in moving forward. The *Study Guide* is demanding by virtue of the seriousness of the task, and each lesson requires between three to five hours of preparation. In addition, most lessons require about an hour and a half for the mentoring elder and mentoree to review and discuss the mentoree's work.

The *Study Guide* is not designed to be a general leadership training manual. It is a specialized leadership training course intended only for those who aspire to be pastor elders and for the congregation's emerging elders, as surfaced by its current elders. Churches should provide other specific leadership training for all leaders and ministry directors.

THE ROLE OF THE *STUDY GUIDE* IN PREPARING ELDERS

The *Study Guide to Biblical Eldership* is designed to provide prospective elders with three crucial elements:

1.   A thorough study of what the Bible teaches about elders and eldering

An often neglected but critically essential requirement for training new elders is the study of the biblical texts on eldership and Christian leadership. The *Study Guide* directs the trainee through all the New Testament passages on eldership, using *Biblical Eldership* as an in-depth commentary. Lesson 1 begins with Old Testament elders (chapter 7 of *Biblical Eldership*). The *Guide* then moves through Acts (also chapter 7), followed by all the epistles (chapters 8-13). The *Study Guide* also refers to the first six chapters of *Biblical Eldership* as they relate to the eldership texts of Scripture. Therefore, **before starting lesson 1 of the *Study Guide*, the mentoree should read the introduction and the first six chapters of *Biblical Eldership*.**

Only the Spirit of God, using the Word of God, can instill in the hearts and minds of men God's will for what they should be and do as shepherds of God's precious flock. Therefore, an elder trainee needs to saturate his mind with God-breathed words on biblical eldership. Only when he is "constantly nourished on the words of the faith and of the sound doctrine" will he be "a good servant of Christ Jesus" (1 Tim. 4:6).

2.   Practical ideas for developing prospective elders' pastoral skills and personal spiritual growth

Elder trainees need much practical instruction in preparing for eldership. Since *Biblical Eldership* is largely a doctrinal, expository book, it offers little practical counsel for prospective elders. The *Study Guide* supplements *Biblical Eldership* by providing probing questions, self-evaluations, assignments, useful suggestions, and recommended reading material.

Throughout the *Study Guide*, many books are recommended for study or purchase as resource material. Mentorees may not be able to afford such an investment, so we suggest that the church purchase these books for an elders' resource library. It is important that basic books are at hand for training leaders and elders.

To maximize the trainee's practical experience, it will be helpful if he is allowed to attend elders' meetings while he is working on these lessons. Elders' meetings are an extraordinarily effective training ground for emerging elders. They are a virtual school of advanced pastoral training. Observing experienced leaders is fundamental to the mentoring process. While training the Twelve, Jesus was the model. He provided maximum exposure for His disciples to observe His methods of evangelism, the priority of prayer in His life, His compassion for suffering people, His leadership style, and His absolute faithfulness to the will and Word of God. The more exposure the mentoree has to the elders at work, the more effective the mentoring process will be. In addition, trainees should seek opportunities to accompany the elders in their pastoral duties. In-service training is always effective.

3.   **A guide to facilitate a mentoring relationship between an experienced elder and an elder trainee**

If a church is blessed with a well-trained council of elders, the *Study Guide* provides an organized format to be used by elders in mentoring men preparing to share that responsibility in the future. This *Guide* provides the structure for a mentoring elder and mentoree to study all the biblical texts on elders and the book *Biblical Eldership*. It also allows the mentoring elder to share his personal insights into Scripture; his personal spiritual journey and growth; and his experiences, failures, and successes as a shepherd of God's people.

Please be aware that a number of assignments and questions may require much more effort than the lesson schedule allows. List these items at the back of the *Guide* under *Future Assignments and Discussions*. When you complete the *Study Guide*, prioritize the postponed items and schedule time to work on each.

SUGGESTIONS FOR AN EFFECTIVE MENTORING RELATIONSHIP

So that you may derive the greatest benefit from your mentoring relationship, we recommend that both the mentoring elder and the trainee read the book, *Connecting: The Mentoring Relationships You Need To Succeed in Life,* by Paul D. Stanley and J. Robert Clinton. It is available from your local bookstore or from Lewis & Roth (800-477-3239). It is without question the finest book available on spiritual mentoring. Stanley and Clinton briefly define mentoring as "a relational experience through which one person empowers another by sharing God-given resources."[6] Their expanded definition reads:

> Mentoring is a relational process between [a] mentor, who knows or has experienced something and transfers that something (resources of wisdom, information, experience, confidence, insight, relationships, status, etc.) to a mentoree, at an appropriate time and manner, so that it facilitates development or empowerment.[7]

Stanley and Clinton dispel false ideas about mentoring and challenge us to seek different kinds of mentoring relationships throughout life for our continued growth.

In a church with several capable elders, one elder does not have to mentor a trainee through all twelve lessons of the *Guide*. As Stanley and Clinton explain, there is no one "ideal," or "all-encompassing mentor" for each of us for life,[8] so different elders should be involved with the trainee in specific areas of mentoring.

> When seeking a mentor, don't look for an ideal person who can do the whole range of mentoring functions. Few of these exist, if any. But if the mentoring needs are specified, someone is usually available who can mentor to that need. We believe that mentors are part of God's development plan for each of His followers. He will provide them as you "ask and seek."[9]

An elder who is more doctrinally astute should mentor prospective elders in the importance of knowing Bible doctrine (lessons 2, 4, and 8), for example, while an elder who is gifted in counseling and ministering to families should cover lesson 7. An elder who is devoted to prayer should guide the mentoree through lesson 3. This gives trainees the opportunity to learn from several mentoring elders and to draw from their particular strengths, experience, and gifts. However, one elder should be the primary mentoring elder for the trainee in order to provide close accountability for the overall training.

Mentoring should not end when a man becomes a pastor elder. The best learning actually occurs when one is in the process of serving. Furthermore, new elders need the closest mentoring. They need on-the-job training, guidance, counsel, rebuke, correction, love, and encouragement. Since the first few years as a pastor elder are the most strategic for growth in his shepherding ministry, it is imperative that experienced elders seize this opportunity to deliberately pass on their wisdom, knowledge, and skills to their new colleagues. In this way, the eldership is successfully perpetuated, guaranteeing future pastoral care for the local church.

---

[1] Steve Huntley, with Jeannye Thornton, "The Silent Strength of Family Businesses," *U. S. News & World Report* (April 25, 1983), p. 47.

[2] Ibid., p. 50.

[3] Kenneth O. Gangel, *Feeding and Leading* (Wheaton: Victor, 1989), p. 313.

[4] Ibid., p. 309.

[5] A. B. Bruce, *The Training of the Twelve* (1871; reprinted Grand Rapids: Kregel, 1988), pp. 12, 13. Descriptions and dates are provided in this *Guide* only for those authors not previously identified in *Biblical Eldership*.

[6] Paul D. Stanley and J. Robert Clinton, *Connecting: The Mentoring Relationships You Need To Succeed in Life* (Colorado Springs: NavPress, 1992), p. 33.

[7] Ibid., p. 40.

[8] Ibid., pp. 45, 46.

[9] Ibid., p. 45.

ELDER QUALIFICATIONS

1 Timothy 3:2-7	**Titus 1:6-9**	**1 Peter 5:1-3**
1. Above reproach	1. Above reproach	1. Not shepherding under compulsion, but voluntarily
2. The husband of one wife	2. The husband of one wife	2. Not shepherding for sordid gain, but with eagerness
3. Temperate [self-controlled, balanced]	3. Having children who believe	3. Not lording it over the flock, but proving to be an example
4. Prudent [sensible, good judgment]	4. Not self-willed	
5. Respectable [well-behaved, virtuous]	5. Not quick-tempered	
6. Hospitable	6. Not addicted to wine	
7. Able to teach	7. Not pugnacious	
8. Not addicted to wine	8. Not fond of sordid gain	
9. Not pugnacious [not belligerent]	9. Hospitable	
10. Gentle [forbearing]	10. Lover of what is good [kind, virtuous]	
11. Peaceable [uncontentious]	11. Sensible [see prudent]	
12. Free from the love of money	12. Just [righteous conduct, law-abiding]	
13. Manages his household well	13. Devout [holy, pleasing to God, loyal to His Word]	
14. Not a new convert	14. Self-controlled	
15. A good reputation with those outside the church	15. Holds fast the faithful [trustworthy NIV] Word, both to exhort and to refute	

LESSON 1

OLD TESTAMENT ELDERS

LESSON OVERVIEW

Every prospective shepherd elder needs good role models to learn from and to follow. God's book, the Bible, provides us with many inspiring examples of godly men and women. In their excellent book on mentoring, Paul Stanley and Robert Clinton call such an example an "Historical Model," meaning "a person now dead whose life or ministry is written in a(n) (auto)biographical form and is used as an example to indirectly impart values, principles, and skills that empower another person."[1]

Lesson 1 explores Job's life as a model of the Old Testament elder. We will examine the duties and deficiencies of Israel's elders and will note the failure of Job's colleagues to compassionately and tactfully minister to him during his intense suffering. This lesson will help you think and act like a biblical, Christlike elder.

JOB, A MODEL ELDER

"There was a man in the land of Uz whose name was Job, and that man was blameless, upright, fearing God and turning away from evil." Job 1:1

Read pages 186-202, 227-238. It is assumed that you have previously read pages 9-117.

---

1. Using a Bible dictionary, encyclopedia, or other reference tool,[2] briefly describe who Job is and what the book of Job is about.

   A wealthy man of upright character & devoted to God. Yet God allows Satan to test Job by taking away everything even his family. Job refuses to give up on God & His faithfulness, even amidst friends telling him to curse God & die

2. The verses below describe Job's personal character traits and his actions as a community leader.

    a. As you read each passage, mark with an **"E"** each reference that substantiates that Job was an elder.

    b. Where appropriate, summarize what Job did that a shepherd elder should do.

     c. Consider the New Testament qualifications of an elder on the list below and, using the numbers **1** through **11** that correspond to those qualifications, identify each passage that contains similar qualifications.

       1   **Above reproach** (1 Tim. 3:2; pp. 188, 228)

       2   **Hospitable** (1 Tim. 3:2; p. 194)

       3   **Respectable** [well-behaved, virtuous] (1 Tim. 3:3; p. 193)

       4   **Gentle** [forbearing] (1 Tim 3:3; p. 197)

       5   **Free from the love of money** (1 Tim. 3:3; p. 198)

       6   **Manages his household well** (1 Tim. 3:4; p. 199)

       7   **Lover of what is good** [kind, virtuous] (Titus 1:8; p. 233)

       8   **Just** [righteous conduct, law-abiding] (Titus 1:8; p. 234)

       9   **Devout** [holy, pleasing to God, loyal to His Word] (Titus 1:8; p. 235)

     10   **Faithful to God's Word** (Titus 1:9; pp. 235, 236)

     11   **Able to teach and exhort, and to refute false teachers** (Titus 1:9; pp. 236, 237)

Job 1:1 There was a man in the land of Uz whose name was Job, and that man was blameless, upright, fearing God and turning away from evil.

Example: b. Job was blameless, God-fearing; c. 1, 8, 9

Job 1:4, 5 And his sons used to go and hold a feast in the house of each one on his day, and they would send and invite their three sisters to eat and drink with them. It came about, when the days of feasting had completed their cycle, that Job would send and consecrate them, rising up early in the morning and offering burnt offerings according to the number of them all; for Job said, "Perhaps my sons have sinned and cursed God in their hearts." Thus Job did continually.

Job 4:1-4 Then Eliphaz the Temanite answered, "If one ventures a word with you [Job], will you become impatient? But who can refrain from speaking? Behold you [Job] have admonished [instructed] many, and you have strengthened weak hands. Your words have helped the tottering to stand, and you have strengthened feeble knees."

Job 23:11, 12 "My foot [Job's] has held fast to His path; I have kept His way and not turned aside. I have not departed from the command of His lips; I have treasured the words of His mouth more than my necessary food."

Job 29:7, 8 "When I [Job] went out to the gate of the city, when I took my seat in the square, the young men saw me and hid themselves, and the old men arose and stood."

Job 29:12-17 "Because I delivered the poor who cried for help, and the orphan who had no helper. The blessing of the one ready to perish came upon me, and I made the widow's heart sing for joy. I put on righteousness, and it clothed me; my justice was like a robe and a turban. I was eyes to the blind and feet to the lame. I was a father to the needy, and I investigated the case which I did not know. I broke the jaws of the wicked and snatched the prey from his teeth."

Job 29:21 "To me they listened and waited, and kept silent for my counsel."

Job 30:25 "Have I not wept for the one whose life is hard? Was not my soul grieved for the needy?"

Job 31:1 "I have made a covenant with my eyes; how then could I gaze [look lustfully *NIV*] at a virgin?"

Job 31:24-34 "If I have put my confidence in gold, and called fine gold my trust, if I have gloated because my wealth was great, and because my hand had secured so much; if I have looked at the sun when it shone or the moon going in splendor, and my heart became secretly enticed, and my hand threw a kiss from my mouth, that too would have been an iniquity calling for judgment, for I would have denied God above. Have I rejoiced at the extinction of my enemy, or exulted when evil befell him? No, I have not allowed my mouth to sin by asking for his life in a curse. Have the men of my tent not said, 'Who can find one who has not been satisfied with his meat'? The alien has not lodged outside, for I have opened my doors to the traveler. Have I covered my transgressions like Adam, by hiding my iniquity in my bosom, because I feared the great multitude, and the contempt of families terrified me, and kept silent and did not go out of doors?"

3. In summary, what was Job's attitude toward people? *he loved people (both physical needs, mental needs, spiritual needs, social, etc...)*

The following observation is from a letter by Hudson Taylor, founder of the China Inland Mission and one of the greatest missionaries of all time. He wrote about the lack of tact and sensitivity some missionaries displayed toward the Chinese. May his words remind us of the importance of grace and tact in dealing with people:

"Some persons seem really clever in doing the right thing in the worst possible way, or at the most unfortunate time. Really dull, or rude persons will seldom be out of hot water in China; and though earnest and clever and pious will not effect much. *In nothing do we fail more, as a Mission, than in lack of tact and politeness.*"
                                                                                                      Hudson Taylor[3]

---

 4. Job complained that his five friends, who may also have been elders, were miserable comforters. **"You are all worthless physicians"** (Job 13:4). **"Sorry comforters are you all"** (Job 16:2). Many elders today think and act like Job's friends. So that you will not become a worthless physician of the soul, observe the negative characteristics in Job's friends that shepherds of God's people should avoid. List those that appear in these passages.

Job 6:14, 15 "For the despairing man [Job speaking] there should be kindness from his friend; so that he does not forsake the fear of the Almighty. My brothers [Job's friends] have acted deceitfully like a wadi [a seasonal stream], like the torrents of wadis which vanish."

Example: lack of compassion, inconsistent, useless

Job 12:5a "He who is at ease holds calamity in contempt."

Job 13:4 "But you smear with lies; you are all worthless physicians."

Job 16:1-4 Then Job answered, "I have heard many such things; sorry comforters are you all. Is there no limit to windy words? Or what plagues you that you answer? I too could speak like you, if I were in your place. I could compose words against you and shake my head at you."

Job 19:1-5 Then Job responded, "How long will you torment me, and crush me with words? These ten times you have insulted me; you are not ashamed to wrong me. . . . If indeed you vaunt yourselves against me, and prove my disgrace to me."

5. Restate Job 12:5*a* in your own words. Why is it important for those who provide spiritual care to understand and remember this text?

chaos (calamity) lack of order is the enemy of those who desire true peace (ease)

ISRAEL'S ELDERS

"And they [the elders] shall bear the burden of the people with you." Numbers 11:17

Read pages 121-124.

6. Practice pronouncing the following Greek words, and give their meanings:

presbyteros [prez BOO tuh rohs] (p. 124)

presbyteroi [prez BOO tuh roy] (p. 124)

presbyterion [prez boo TEH ree ohn] (pp. 123, 205)

gerousia [geh roo SEE uh] (p. 123)

7. Briefly define the eldership structure of government of the Old Testament (p. 39).

 8. The divinely inspired New Testament is built on the divinely inspired Old Testament. A major reason why most Christians do not see or understand church eldership as practiced in the New Testament is that they do not know anything about the Old Testament elders. Robert B. Girdlestone (1836-1923), author of the classic *Synonyms of the Old Testament*, echoes this sentiment: "The importance of a right judgment of the position and functions of these [Old Testament] elders cannot well be overrated when we come to discuss the nature of the analogous office of presbyter in the NT."[4]

Elders appear throughout the entire Bible, beginning with Genesis 50:7 and ending with Revelation 4:4, which describes the twenty-four elders who surround the throne of God. Since government by a council of elders has been a fundamental institution among the people of God all through biblical history, a study of New Testament church eldership must begin with an examination of what the Old Testament says about elders.

List the responsibilities of the elders of Israel indicated in these Old Testament passages. Be sure to interpret these verses in their context.

Ex. 19:7, 8

Lev. 4:13-15

Num. 11:16, 17

Deut. 19:11, 12

Deut. 21:18-21

Deut. 27:1

Deut. 31:9-12

2 Sam. 5:3

Job 12:20

Ezek. 7:26

9. Although today's elders do not offer sacrifices, protect manslayers, or sit at the city gate, there are important similarities between the responsibilities of the Old and New Testament elders. List some of these similarities.

10. What highly significant lesson for elders do you find in Joshua 24:31?

Israel served the Lord throughout Joshua's life & the elders that served under him — they continually honored God
→ After Joshua's leaders died, what then?
— Cultivate future leaders —
— As go the elders/ leaders, so goes the church

11. By and large, Israel's elders failed to meet their responsibility to uphold the law of God and protect the people. We also cannot assume that collective leadership will protect us from the consequences of corporate sin.

What were some of the root sins and failures of Israel's elders? Again, be sure to observe the context.

1 Sam. 4:1-11 *— using the "Ark" as their trust rather than God*

1 Sam. 8:4-9, 19, 20 *trusting in "Kings" rather than God*

1 Sam. 11:1-3 gave into fear of a leader

2 Sam. 5:3; 17:1-4 broke the covenant

1 Kings 21:5-11 afraid of the powerful

Ezek. 8:7-13 led into idolatry

12. In light of your desire to become a godly leader or elder, write brief phrases that summarize the biblical standards for character and conduct for elders that you have gleaned from this study.

I must:

a. stay faithful to God in all circumstances.

b. love/serve all people, regardless of status or what they can offer to me

c. be devout / faithful to God's Holy Word

d. manage my family in all of life's circumstances.
   ↳ train them in the good & in the bad.

e. have respected character

f. watch that money doesn't control me

g. be a ongoing student of God's Word & able to teach

h.

i.

j.

k.

l.

m.

n.

o.

Scripture Memory Assignment:

"There was a man in the land of Uz whose name was Job; and that man was blameless, upright, fearing God and turning away from evil."
                                                                        Job 1:1

---

[1] Paul D. Stanley and J. Robert Clinton, *Connecting: The Mentoring Relationship You Need to Succeed in Life* (Colorado Springs: NavPress, 1992), p. 147.

[2] We highly recommend that every elder own and use regularly *Talk Thru the Bible,* by Bruce Wilkinson and Kenneth Boa (Nashville: Thomas Nelson Publishers). For a good Bible dictionary, we recommend the *New Bible Dictionary,* by Tyndale House Publishers.

[3] A. J. Broomhall, *Refiner's Fire* (Robesonia: The Overseas Missionary Fellowship, 1985), p. 231.

[4] Robert Baker Girdlestone, *Synonyms of the Old Testament*, 3d ed. (Grand Rapids: Baker, 1983), p. 269.

LESSON 2

MEN OF SOUND DOCTRINE AND WISDOM

LESSON OVERVIEW

Although there are important similarities between Old and New Testament elders, it would be a mistake to consider the apostolic elder to be simply the Old Testament elder in a new era. To try to define the New Testament elder (Pauline elder) in terms of the Old Testament elder or the Jewish synagogue elder (of whom we know very little) is to distort the New Testament's teachings on eldership. The work and qualifications of the Christian elder are more clearly defined than those of the Old Testament elder. In the following eleven lessons, we will study the New Testament elder and work through the implications of these teachings for your own ministry.

Lesson 2 sets forth the biblical imperative that elders know Bible doctrine so that they will be adequately equipped to judge doctrinal disputes and provide wise, godly counsel and leadership for the congregation. As you will discover throughout the *Guide*, biblical elders must be men of the Word. The biblical standard for pastor elders is that they be able to teach and defend sound Christian doctrine. Elders who are biblically inadequate are actually a curse to the church, not the blessing God would have them be. This lesson is intended to help you evaluate your preparedness as a teacher and defender of Christ's doctrine. It will also touch briefly on the elder-congregation relationship and the need for elders to be men of wisdom who know how to lead the congregation in godly decision making.

JUDGING DOCTRINAL ISSUES

"Some men came down from Judea and began teaching the brethren, 'Unless you are circumcised according to the custom of Moses, you cannot be saved.' And when Paul and Barnabas had great dissension and debate with them, the brethren determined that Paul and Barnabas and some others of them should go up to Jerusalem to the apostles and elders concerning this issue." Acts 15:1, 2

Review pages 17-22. Read pages 125-133, 291-295.

1. Do not be surprised by doctrinal controversy. The first Christians struggled over doctrinal issues. Even the apostles' presence did not prevent theological conflict. As we see in Acts 15, it

is the elders' responsibility to deal with doctrinal controversy. Elders must be able to judge opposing theological views, weigh arguments, discern error, deal with potentially explosive situations, arbitrate, and make sound, expeditious decisions.

a. Should maintaining peace within the church always be the elder's goal? Support your answer from Paul's actions in Acts 15:1, 2.

b. According to Acts 15, what was the chief doctrinal issue debated by these first Christians?

c. Outline the process used by the church in Jerusalem to resolve the controversy.

d. What do we learn from the fact that the apostles did not settle this doctrinal issue with a simple, authoritative, apostolic decree, without debate and congregational involvement?

    e.   Contrast Paul's attitude toward those who opposed him as recorded in Acts 15:1, 2; Gal. 1:6-9, 2:4-5; and 2:11-16, with his opinions recorded in Phil. 1:15-18. Compare with Mark 9:38-41. What determined the differences? What principles can you learn from this?

2.   Select those elder qualifications that qualify elders to judge and resolve doctrinal conflict in a Christian manner and explain your reason for each selection. You may include several qualifications in a single explanation where appropriate.

1 Timothy 3:2-7

1. Above reproach
2. The husband of one wife
3. Temperate [self-controlled, balanced]
4. Prudent [sensible, good judgment]
5. Respectable [well-behaved, virtuous]
6. Hospitable
7. Able to teach
8. Not addicted to wine
9. Not pugnacious [not belligerent]
10. Gentle [forbearing]
11. Peaceable [uncontentious]
12. Free from the love of money
13. Manages his household well
14. Not a new convert
15. A good reputation with those outside the church

Titus 1:6-9

1. Above reproach
2. The husband of one wife
3. Having children who believe
4. Not self-willed
5. Not quick-tempered
6. Not addicted to wine
7. Not pugnacious
8. Not fond of sordid gain
9. Hospitable
10. Lover of what is good [kind, virtuous]
11. Sensible [see prudent]
12. Just [righteous conduct, law-abiding]
13. Devout [holy, pleasing to God, loyal to His Word]
14. Self-controlled
15. Holds fast the faithful [trustworthy NIV] Word, both to exhort and to refute

1 Peter 5:1-3

1. Not shepherding under compulsion, but voluntarily
2. Not shepherding for sordid gain, but with eagerness
3. Not lording it over the flock, but proving to be an example

    a.   *Example:* ***Above reproach, respectable:*** *The elder who is not above reproach will be discredited because of peripheral matters and be ineffective in pursuing the critical issues.*

    b.

      c.

      d.

      e.

      f.

      g.

      h.

3. Discuss whether each elder must possess all of these qualifications, or should the elder council as a whole fulfill these requirements?

4. In order for you to qualify as a pastor elder, God requires that you be able to teach and exhort "in sound doctrine" and refute false doctrine (Titus 1:9). An elder who does not know the doctrines of Scripture is as useful as a lifeguard who does not know how to swim. P. T. Forsyth was right on target when he wrote, "The real strength of the Church is not the amount of its work but the quality of its faith. One man who truly knows his Bible is worth more to the Church's real strength than a crowd of workers who do not."[1]

When elders who have not attended seminary defer to seminary-trained pastors when settling doctrinal issues, what are the consequences?

a.

b.

c.

5. Below are the major Bible doctrines you must know in order to teach and defend "sound doctrine." Indicate after each of the eight doctrines whether or not you are currently prepared to teach and defend it.

   a. **BIBLIOLOGY,** the doctrine of the Bible: general and special revelation; the inspiration, infallibility, canonicity, illumination, and interpretation of the Bible.

   b. **THEOLOGY PROPER,** the doctrine of God: the existence, attributes, and decrees of God; the Trinity.

   c. **CHRISTOLOGY,** the doctrine of Christ: the divine-human natures of Christ and the hypostatic union; the offices and present ministry of Christ; the theophanies and prophecies of Christ.

   d. **PNEUMATOLOGY,** the doctrine of the Holy Spirit: the personality and deity of the Holy Spirit; the Spirit's work in relation to Christ and in regenerating, baptizing, indwelling, gifting, and helping believers.

   e. **SOTERIOLOGY,** the doctrine of salvation: the death of Christ, substitution, propitiation, reconciliation, justification by faith alone, regeneration, election, free will, grace, faith, perseverance.

   f. **ANTHROPOLOGY AND HARMARTIOLOGY,** the doctrines of man and sin: the origin, fall, and nature of man; the definition of sin and imputation of sin.

   g. **ECCLESIOLOGY,** the doctrine of the church: the relationship between Israel and the Church; the local church and the universal Church; the imagery used to describe the church (body, bride, priesthood, temple, flock); the government of the church; the ordinances of the church; evangelism, spiritual gifts, and ministry.

   h. **ESCHATOLOGY,** the doctrine of last things: heaven, hell, return and rule of Christ, resurrection, judgment, and man's eternal state.

6. As an elder, you will work with people who hold differing theological views. When is tolerance appropriate, and when is it necessary to challenge a teaching as false and harmful to the church? Keep in mind that scriptural data for some doctrines is inconclusive, and faithful scholars who are committed to the authority of Scripture have disagreed on such doctrines throughout church history. However, on essential matters Scripture is clear, and adherence to these teachings is crucial to the spiritual health of the church.

   a. There are essential doctrines that are not negotiable and on which we will not compromise. List several examples.

   b. There are other doctrinal issues on which we must agree to disagree. List several examples of such issues that are treated this way in your church.

7. The suggested resources and practical methods below can help you enhance your knowledge of Bible doctrine. Record your decisions as to which of these you need to invest in or implement in order to become doctrinally equipped to shepherd God's flock.

   a. For a basic introductory book on the foundational doctrines of Christianity, read *Know What You Believe: A Practical Discussion of the Fundamentals of the Christian Faith*, by Paul E. Little.[2] Also highly recommended is Little's companion volume, *Know Why You Believe.*[3]

   For more advanced study, read *The Moody Handbook of Theology,* by Paul Enns.[4] Enns's book is an excellent reference tool even if you do not entirely agree with his theology. Elders should own basic reference tools for equipping themselves and for answering the biblical and doctrinal questions directed to them.

   b. For a systematic study of doctrine, start with *Decide for Yourself: A Theological Workbook,* by Gordon R. Lewis.[5] Lewis presents all the Scripture passages on each of the major doctrines, but requires that you work out your own conclusions. You will find that this book is an invaluable tool for studying Bible doctrine.

   c. Develop your own topical, Bible doctrine workbook. Add to this as you regularly read the Bible (see the next lesson). For example, when you find a passage that teaches Christ's divine nature, note the verse that refers to His deity on the workbook page designated "Christology - Divine Nature." Your notebook will be an excellent resource for quickly locating passages needed for teaching and answering questions.

    d.   Teaching tapes are one of the most efficient tools for using time wisely and maintaining consistent growth in your knowledge of the Word and doctrine. Many men use the time they spend exercising or driving to listen to great Bible expositors teach the Scriptures. This will amount to many hours of Bible teaching over the years.

        A number of churches that are well-known for their Bible teachers loan or give away teaching tapes. We always encourage churches and men to regularly order such series and urge them to start with a set on the book of Romans. It is absolutely essential that church leaders master the book of Romans because it represents the most systematic statement of Christian doctrine found in Scripture.

    e.   Study theology or Bible through a reputable correspondence school. If you are able, take a theology course at a local Bible school or seminary.

Document your plans for further study and discuss them with your mentor.

8.   What arguments presented in *Biblical Eldership* refute James Bannerman's claim that Acts 15 supports the *necessity* for an ecclesiastical court that rules over the local church (pp. 125-130)? Bannerman asserts:

    Now, in this narrative we have all the elements necessary to make up the idea of a supreme ecclesiastical court, with authority over not only the members and office-bearers within the local bounds of the congregations represented, but also the Presbyteries or inferior Church courts included in the same limits (p. 128).

    a.

b.

c.

ELDERS AND THE CONGREGATION

"And the following day Paul went in with us to James, and all the elders were present. . . . And they said to him, 'You see, brother, how many thousands there are among the Jews of those who have believed, and they are all zealous for the Law; and they have been told about you, that you are teaching all the Jews who are among the Gentiles to forsake Moses, telling them not to circumcise their children nor to walk according to the customs. What, then, is to be done? They will certainly hear that you have come. Therefore do this that we tell you.'"
Acts 21:18, 20b-23a

> **Review pages 291-295.**

9. The several meetings recorded in Acts 15 are important examples of how church leaders and congregations should meet together to resolve doctrinal problems. List the biblical obligations the elders have to the congregation and those the congregation has to its elders.

    a.   The elders' obligations to the congregation:

    Titus 1:7

    1 Peter 5:3

    Acts 20:28

b. The congregation's obligations to its elders:

1 Thess. 5:12, 13

1 Tim. 5:17

Heb. 13:7

Heb. 13:17

1 Tim. 5:19, 20

1 Tim. 3:10; cf. **1 Tim. 5:22**

1 Thess. 5:25

10. In leading their congregation so that it will make wise corporate decisions, church leaders must recognize and avoid certain dangers. What are these dangers? See pp. 293-295.

11. What are the key steps church leaders must take in order to lead the congregation in good decision making?

   a.

   b.

   c.

   d.

   e.

   f.

   g.

PROVIDING COUNSEL AND RESOLVING CONFLICT

"Appoint elders in every city as I directed you, namely, if any man is . . . . able both to exhort in sound doctrine and to refute those who contradict. For there are many rebellious men, empty talkers and deceivers, especially those of the circumcision, who must be silenced because they are upsetting whole families, teaching things they should not teach for the sake of sordid gain."   Titus 1:5*b*, 6*a*, 9*b*-11

"Be diligent to present yourself approved to God as a workman who does not need to be ashamed, accurately handling the word of truth."   2 Timothy 2:15

| **Review pages 130-133.** |
---

12. What problems, created by Paul's presence in Jerusalem, were the Jerusalem elders trying to resolve? See Acts 21:18-25.

"It is impossible to lead anyone without facing opposition. The leader must learn to take the heat. He will face opposition–it's an occupational hazard of every leader."   Charles Swindoll[6]

13. Do you agree with the recommendations of the Jerusalem elders, or do you believe they acted improperly, out of fear? Why?

14. What does the apostle Paul's submission to the decision of the elders tell us about the governance of the church?

15. In Acts 15, the Jerusalem elders had to counsel Paul on how to quell false rumors and resolve potential division over his presence in Jerusalem. Draw from the following verses those characteristics that are necessary in the man who would be a wise, godly counselor.

    Ps. 119:97-100

    Prov. 1:7

    Prov. 3:5-7

    Prov. 4:6-9

    Prov. 11:2

    Prov. 16:21

    Prov. 29:20

    Acts 6:3

    James 3:17, 18

16. Is there any other quality, not listed in your answers above, that is important in counseling and resolving conflict? Explain why.

ASSIGNMENT:

Review your church's doctrinal statement. Discuss with your mentoring elder the church's doctrinal distinctives and any relevant history. Question him as to differences of opinion on doctrinal issues that will be tolerated by the elder council. Review any reservations you have concerning the doctrinal statement and devise a study plan to resolve them.

SCRIPTURE MEMORY ASSIGNMENT

"Be diligent to present yourself approved to God as a workman who does not need to be ashamed, accurately handling the word of truth."   2 Timothy 2:15

---

[1] P. T. Forsyth, *The Church and the Sacraments* (1917; repr. London: Independent, 1955), p. 9.

[2] Paul E. Little, *Know What You Believe: A Practical Discussion of the Fundamentals of the Christian Faith* (Wheaton: Victor Books, 1987).

[3] Paul E. Little, *Know Why You Believe* (Downers Grove: InterVarsity Press, 1988).

[4] Paul Enns, *The Moody Handbook of Theology* (Chicago: Moody Press, 1989). An additional resource is Charles C. Ryrie, *Basic Theology: A Popular Systematic Guide To Understanding Biblical Truth* (Wheaton: Victor Books, 1987).

[5] Gordon R. Lewis, *Decide for Yourself: A Theological Workbook* (Downers Grove: InterVarsity, 1970).

[6] Charles Swindoll, *Hand Me Another Brick* (Nashville: Thomas Nelson, 1978), p. 78.

LESSON 3

THE FIRST ELDER APPOINTMENTS
"GUARD YOURSELVES"

LESSON OVERVIEW

In this lesson we will be confronted by the significance of Acts 14:23 to the New Testament doctrine of eldership and learn to think accurately about the Greek word for "appointed," which is frequently misinterpreted to mean church election or ordination.

Most of the lesson covers Acts 20:28*a*: "Be on guard for yourselves." Shepherds cannot guard others from Satan's many deceptions if they do not first guard their own souls. This lesson reinforces the Lord's call for us to be men of the Word and of prayer.

THE FIRST ELDER APPOINTMENTS

"When they had appointed elders for them in every church, having prayed with fasting, they commended them to the Lord in whom they had believed." Acts 14:23

| Read pages 133-140. |
---

1. What unique contributions does Acts 14:23 make to the subject of eldership?

   a. each single church had elders appointed

   b. the church commended the appointed elders

   c. the church prayed & fasted

   d.

   e.

2. What errors are commonly made when translating the Greek verb *cheirotoneō*, which means "appointed"?

   a.

   b.

3. Some scholars and denominations teach that Paul and Barnabas merely presided over each church's election of its elders. Carefully study the Greek word *cheirotoneō* and its context. In your own words, summarize the points made in *Biblical Eldership* for rejecting the view that Paul and Barnabas only supervised the congregation's election of elders. If you find it too difficult to understand some of these technical linguistic points, find someone to help you.

   a. Philo (Jewish philosopher) uses the word c̄ reference to voting

   b. the New Testament used it in a compound form to mean "chosen before by God"

   c. "they" appointed refers to Paul & Barnabas

   d. Paul & Barnabas appoints for "them", Not by them

   e. "they" commended "them" / ∞ elders entrusted c̄ them

4. What fundamental spiritual lesson did Barnabas and Paul teach the new Galatian believers by their act of praying with fasting before they entrusted the elders to God's care in the apostles' absence? See pp. 153-156.

"GUARD YOURSELVES"

"'Be on guard for yourselves.'"   Acts 20:28*a*

"Pay close attention to yourself and to your teaching; persevere in these things, for as you do this you will insure salvation both for yourself and for those who hear you."   1 Timothy 4:16

"'But we will devote ourselves to prayer and to the ministry of the word.'"   Acts 6:4

"A good servant of Christ Jesus [is] constantly nourished on the words of the faith and of the sound doctrine."   1 Timothy 4:6*b*

"Now He was telling them a parable to show that at all times they ought to pray and not to lose heart."   Luke 18:1

Read pages 140-147.

Before a shepherd elder can guard God's flock from the enemy, *he must first be able to guard his own inner spiritual life.* In Paul's message to the Ephesian elders, he exhorts them to guard themselves from enemy attack first, then to guard the flock. To guard yourself spiritually–among other spiritual disciplines–you must cultivate a consistent life pattern of Bible reading, study, meditation, and prayer. This is especially important because elders are to dedicate themselves to prayer and the Word (Acts 6:4).

THE ELDER AND THE WORD

5. Study how Paul instructs Timothy to guard himself in 2 Timothy 3:13-17. List what this passage teaches the shepherd of God's flock.

Realise:

a. *evil will go from bad to worse*

b. *All scripture is inspired by God*

c. *to teach*

d. *rebuke*

e. *correcting, training in righteousness*

f.

God's Word will be your primary weapon for protecting the flock, so you must know it well and be able to use it. It is also your personal source of incredible spiritual strength, wisdom, and encouragement. That is why, at the end of his farewell, Paul commended the Ephesian elders "to God and to the word of His grace" (Acts 20:32). Only God and His living, breathing Word could sustain these elders through the fierce storms that lay ahead. Therefore, a godly elder must be a *man of the Book*! He must be a *Word-filled* and *Word-controlled* believer. With the Psalmist, a godly elder says, "O how I love Your law! It is my meditation all the day" (Ps. 119:97).

Unfortunately, in our hyperactive, overly busy society, regular, meditative reading of the Bible is often neglected. John Stott points out the paradox:

> This much purchased book is a much neglected book. Probably tens of thousands of people who buy the Bible never read it. Even in churches, knowledge of the Bible is abysmal. Few church members make a practice of daily Bible meditation.[1]

In a sermon to his congregation, S. Lewis Johnson remonstrates:

> I have come to believe . . . that the great sin of Christians in evangelical churches is neglect of the Bible. It has been my observation, and I am including myself, that our greatest failure is that we don't read the Bible. We listen to people talk about the Bible. We listen to preachers like me, and we read books, but we do not read the Bible.[2]

As a spiritual guide to God's people, the elder must love God's infallible Word. This love for God's Book will be manifested primarily by the elder's desire to read the Bible regularly. A man who has no such desire for the Word is not called of the Spirit to be a shepherd elder. In fact, such a man is a danger to the church.

To become more consistent and productive in reading and meditating on God's precious Word, carefully consider the practical suggestions presented below. *If any of these suggestions will not work for you, state the reason and propose an alternative.*

Use an Accurate Translation of the Bible.

For your regular reading, study, and meditation of Scripture, use a sound, accurate translation of the Hebrew and Greek–not a paraphrase. A paraphrased Bible is good for comprehending the overall context of a passage, but it is not adequate for study and interpretation. In the translation process, choices are made between making the translation easy to read and retaining accuracy. When detailed interpretation is your objective, an accurate translation must be used.

The three most popular Bibles that are based on accurate Hebrew and Greek texts and are used for study and preaching are the New International Version, New American Standard Bible, and New King James Version. Your study Bible will be a useful tool for ten or twenty years. It will become the familiar repository for your own marginal notes, cross-references, and underlined passages. So invest in a high quality Bible with easy-to-read print and adequate margins for notes.

Only the Scripture that you have memorized or can easily find is truly useful to you in most ministry situations. It would be to your advantage to work out a system for indexing passages by theological or counseling subjects so that you can find them quickly at the moment of need.

 6.   Record how you will use your study Bible:

    a.   What Bible is your main study Bible?   *NIV*

    b.   How do you mark key passages?   *underline / highlight*

    c.   If you are keeping a doctrinal subject index, how do you key these passages? Show your mentor how you do this.

Use a Bible-reading Program to Guide You in Your Daily Bible Reading.

Bible reading is different in purpose from detailed Bible study in which we work through a theological issue or prepare to teach. We need to read through the entire Bible in order to understand the scope of redemptive history and learn where specific issues are addressed. Consistent reading of the whole Bible enables us to understand God's mind and is essential to understanding individual passages.

Without a clear plan of action, however, most of us seldom go beyond the good intention stage. Many Christians stumble along for years, reading the Bible haphazardly and inconsistently or not at all. If you believe that regular, disciplined Bible reading is indispensable to personal Christian growth, then you must spend time in the Word on a regular basis.

The secret to a consistent, Bible-reading lifestyle is to have a Bible reading plan that will enable you to realistically and accurately evaluate your time with God in the Word. If you cannot find a Bible reading plan that suits you well, develop your own. Your program should include reading through the New Testament epistles twice a year because the epistles are the heart and soul of the Christian faith; they interpret the rest of Scripture for us.

Meditate on your Scripture reading as an adjunct to prayer. Select a portion of what you have read and, using a 3x5 card to moderate your pace, focus on each word. Do not race through. It is better to read smaller portions of Scripture profitably than to read longer passages with little comprehension and spiritual interaction.

7. What Bible reading plan do you use, and why do you like it? If you do not employ one at present, what is your plan?

Daily Bread Plan ~~Future~~

Schedule Time for Your Bible Reading.

A Puritan preacher once declared, "The Bible is full of infinities and immensities." In truth, the Bible is an extensive document that presents a considerable challenge. If you desire to master God's Word, you must commit to sacrificially spend time reading and studying it. If you do not consciously allocate a portion of your busy day to quietly read and meditate on the Word, this responsibility will remain unmet. Consider the observations of Geoffrey Thomas, in his excellent booklet, *Reading the Bible:*

> For what can be done at any time may be done at no time. So we deliberately create a time to study the Word of God, choosing a part of the day which is set aside for that precious purpose. These moments will not appear as if by magic. Our whole pattern of life must be structured with this time in view.[3]

As to when to read the Scripture, Thomas says,

> Whatever time best suits you when your mind can be free of the clamor of the day and you can concentrate, that period must be guarded jealously. It will often come under attack and we shall find ourselves almost automatically sacrificing it under pressures. Weakness there will mean weakness everywhere, while conversely, strength there brings a strength which will be present in other circumstances. The greatest battles we fight in our Christian lives do not change; we march that familiar terrain of our victories and our set-backs all the years of our pilgrimage. The self-denial required to create a daily time for God's Word is the continued duty of every Christian.[4]

8. Your Bible-reading schedule:

a. Describe your current schedule: *Various N. T. epistles, Proverbs, James, Psalms*

b. Do you intend to improve or change it? *Yes yes*   If so, how? *Planned ~~one~~ one year plan/or 2yr. plan*

Read and Study in a Designated Place.

A very practical matter that is often neglected is finding a conducive place for reading and studying Scripture. Your regular place of study should include a desk, good lighting, pens, paper, highlighters, your Bible, and study tools. Again, listen to the practical advice of Geoffrey Thomas:

> You can take a Bible anywhere, and it is one of the great pleasures of the Christian life to be on a hilltop, or at the seaside, or by a river, reading the Word. But for regular, disciplined reading a place is needed as free from distraction and as conducive to study as possible. Our Saviour went to a garden, Peter had a rooftop and Elijah an upper room. There is an advantage of reading the Scriptures day after day in the place which is firmly associated in your mind with that activity. You can slip into the right frame of mind the moment you sit down, because you have established the habit of getting down to study once you are in that place. Make sure it is well lit. Good light is very important for reading the double columns of a Bible. It should also be properly ventilated and neither too hot nor too cold. The less you are aware of your surroundings while reading, the better.[5]

9. Evaluate your study place:

   a. Where do you study and/or read your Bible?   *Study*

   b. Do you plan to improve your study environment? *some* If so how?

Pray for the Desire and Self-discipline to Read and Study the Bible.

Regular Bible reading is like exercising: we all know we need to do it and we always feel better afterward, but we still neglect it. The reason we fail at regular Bible reading is that we lack self-discipline and strong desire. But discipline is a fruit of the Holy Spirit (Gal. 5:23), and God wants to develop this virtue in your life. Pray that your Father will help you become a more disciplined Christian.

One way to develop a self-disciplined lifestyle is to commit to specific, regular responsibilities that test our progress or failure. Establishing a daily Bible reading program will improve your self-discipline. Initially it is more important to establish regularity than to attempt a large block of time. Start small and increase your time as you succeed. On your days off, spend extra time in God's Word or catch up on your Bible reading program if you have missed a day or two (which happens to all of us).

Remember: disciplined reading and study requires setting priorities and putting family, work, leisure time, television, and sleep in their proper places. Spiritual success does not come without self-sacrifice and discipline.

10. Listed below are some common hindrances to regular Bible reading:

- I have too many other books and magazines to read.
- I have no real desire to read the Bible in a regular, disciplined way.
- I react to Bible reading as a legalistic and mechanical requirement.
- I have a hard time doing anything consistently.
- I don't know how to get started.
- I can't seem to find time to read the Word.
- I find Bible reading unfulfilling and difficult.
- I spend too much time in front of television.

    a. Using this list as an aid, what keeps you from disciplined Bible reading?

* consistently doing anything
* lots of books

    b. What do you propose to remedy or remove these hindrances?

set a daily time & exercise

Learn to Handle Accurately the Word of Truth.

The neglect of Scripture is not the only reason that false teachings infiltrate the church. All cults support their positions by misusing Scripture, so the shepherd elder must know how to accurately interpret Scripture and convincingly correct those who misrepresent the teachings of the Word.

A detailed study of *hermeneutics*, the science of interpretation, is beyond the scope of this *Guide*. However, the fundamental principles of hermeneutics are simple and, if applied, will enable the elder to be "a workman who does not need to be ashamed, accurately handling the word of truth" (2 Tim. 2:15). The proper interpretation of Scripture is based on the following principles:

    a. The authors of Scripture, under the guidance of the Holy Spirit, wrote with the intention that their statements would be understood. Therefore, the natural interpretation that fits the intent or context of the overall passage is the most probable interpretation.

    b. A foundational Protestant principle of biblical interpretation states that the Bible interprets the Bible:

> The infallible rule of interpretation of Scripture is the Scripture itself; and therefore, when there is a question about the true and full sense of any Scripture (which is not manifold, but one), it may be searched and known by other places that speak more clearly.[6]

    c. God revealed Himself over an extended period of history. Therefore, we must use the most recent revelation to interpret the older.

Based on the fact that God has revealed Himself and His will progressively, Edward J. Carnell, in *The Case for Orthodox Theology,*[7] states five summary principles of hermeneutics:

1.   The New Testament interprets the Old Testament.

2.   The Epistles interpret the Gospels.

3.   Systematic passages interpret the incidental.

4.   Universal passages interpret the local.

5.   Didactic passages interpret the symbolic.

A recommended book on hermeneutics is R. C. Sproul's *Knowing Scripture*[8]

THE ELDER'S PRAYER LIFE

Prayer is a major part of the Lord's work, especially for those who lead His people. In fact, it would be more accurate to say, prayer is our work. The disciples made this very clear in Acts 6:4: "'We will devote ourselves to prayer and to the ministry of the word.'" Elders often face perplexing and agonizing situations that cannot be addressed without the Lord's guidance, wisdom, and strength.

Prayer is also absolutely essential to the elder's relationship with Jesus Christ and his personal growth. In *Spiritual Disciplines for the Christian Life*, Donald Whitney points out: "Where there is Godliness there is prayerfulness. Typically picturesque, Spurgeon said it this way: 'Even as the moon influences the tides of the sea, even so does prayer . . . influence the tides of godliness.'"[9]

As important as prayer is to the Christian life, however, few Christians have a consistent, meaningful prayer life. Consider carefully the following statements:

> During the 1980's, more than seventeen thousand members of a major evangelical denomination were surveyed about their prayer habits while attending seminars on prayer for spiritual awakening. Because they attended this kind of seminar, we can assume these people are above average in their interest in prayer. And yet, the surveys revealed that they pray an average of less than five minutes each day. There were two thousand pastors and wives at these same seminars. By their own admission, they pray less than seven minutes a day. It's very easy to make people feel guilty about failure in prayer. . . . But we must come to grips with the fact that to be like Jesus we must pray.
>   Donald S. Whitney[10]

> What is both surprising and depressing is the sheer prayerlessness that characterizes so much of the Western church. It is surprising, because it is out of step with the Bible that portrays what Christian living should be; it is depressing, because it frequently coexists with abounding Christian activity that somehow seems hollow, frivolous, and superficial.
>   D. A. Carson[11]

Jesus never taught his disciples how to preach, only how to pray. He did not speak much of what was needed to preach well, but much of praying well. To know how to speak to God is more than knowing how to speak to man. Not power with men, but power with God is the first thing. Jesus loves to teach us how to pray.

Andrew Murray[12]

When a man is speaking to God he is at his very acme. It is the highest activity of the human soul, and therefore it is at the same time the ultimate test of a man's true spiritual condition. There is nothing that tells the truth about us as Christian people so much as our prayer life. Everything we do in the Christian life is easier than prayer.

D. Martyn Lloyd-Jones[13]

God's will for us is to pray. Prayer is not an option, it is a command. Consider these biblical imperatives:

- "Devote yourselves to prayer" (Col. 4:2*a*).
- "Pray without ceasing" (1 Thess. 5:17).
- "[You] ought to pray and not to lose heart" (Luke 18:1*b*).
- "[Be] devoted to prayer" (Rom. 12:12*c*).
- "Therefore, take up the full armor of God. . . . With all prayer and petition pray at all times in the Spirit, and with this in view, be on the alert with all perseverance and petition for all the saints" (Eph. 6:13*a*, 18).

Meditate on the Word to Motivate and Enrich Your Prayers.

Donald Whitney points out that meditation is the link between Scripture reading and prayer: "We learn to pray by meditating on Scripture for meditation is the missing link between Bible intake and prayer."[14]

Reflect upon this wise counsel from George Müller, one of the strongest men of prayer and faith ever to grace the church of God:

Now what is the food for the inner man? Not prayer, but the Word of God; and here again, not the simple reading of the Word of God, so that it only passes through our minds, just as water passes through a pipe, but considering what we read, pondering over it and applying it to our hearts.

When we pray we speak to God. Now prayer, in order to be continued for any length of time in any other than a formal manner, requires, generally speaking, a measure of strength of godly desire, and the season therefore when this exercise of the soul can be most effectually performed *is after the inner man has been nourished by meditation on the Word of God*, where we find our Father speaking to us, to encourage us, to comfort us, to instruct us, to humble us, to reprove us.[15]

11.   Choose a short passage of Scripture that you have recently used in your meditation time. Write out several thoughts that you derived from the passage and which you were able to turn into prayer.

Planning Is Necessary.

John Piper reminds us of the simple fact that if we want a good prayer life, we must plan for it. Heed what he says:

> Unless I'm badly mistaken, one of the main reasons so many of God's children don't have a significant prayer life is not so much that we don't want to, *but that we don't plan to.* If you want to take a four-week vacation, you don't just get up one summer morning and say, "Hey, let's go today!" You won't have anything ready. You won't know where to go. Nothing has been planned. But that is how many of us treat prayer. We get up day after day and realize that significant times of prayer should be a part of our life, but nothing's ever ready. We don't know where to go. Nothing has been planned. No time. No place. No procedure. And we all know that the opposite of planning is not a wonderful flow of deep, spontaneous experiences in prayer. The opposite of planning is the rut. If you don't plan a vacation you will probably stay home and watch TV. The natural, unplanned flow of spiritual life sinks to the lowest ebb of vitality. There is a race to be run and a fight to be fought. If you want renewal in your life of prayer you must plan to see it.[16]

12.   As is true of your Bible reading, it is essential to set aside a specific time to meet with the Lord in prayer. What is your place and schedule for prayer? *study / throughout the day*
walk through the clinic.

Develop a Prayer Notebook.

People will give prayer requests to their shepherd elders. However, we all have short memories, especially when it comes to remembering prayer requests. If you do not write these requests down, you will often forget them as soon as the next urgent issue comes to your attention. If the shepherd elder takes prayer seriously and considers it part of his spiritual work, he will maintain a notebook. This will help him pray specifically and faithfully.

Revise your prayer notebook often. Reviewing past requests and seeing God's answers will be a great incentive to remain faithful in prayer. Next to your Bible, your prayer notebook is the most important book you have.

13. If you do not already have a prayer notebook, start one. Show it to your mentor, or submit copies of enough pages so that your mentor can see how you organize your notebook, how you record what and who you need to pray for, when you pray about each item, and how you record God's answers.

Use Music to Aid Your Prayers.

For many, music is an excellent aid to prayer. Indeed, singing God's praises is praying. Before you pray, sing or read several hymns, or listen to a music tape. Praising the Lord in song will set the context for your praying.

Try Different Modes for Praying.

It is hard to separate our attitude from our posture. Hudson Taylor found that standing or walking during prayer was the best position for him because it kept his mind from wandering. You could kneel, lie face down, or sit. Or, you can pray out loud as Martin Luther did.

Find a Quiet Place to Pray.

14. What do the following verses teach you about Jesus and prayer?

Mark 1:35 *early in the Am / solitary place*

Mark 6:45, 46 *mountainside*

Luke 5:16 *often went to lonely places*

Luke 6:12 *mountainside, spent the night praying (chose his disciples after)*

Luke 9:18 *private*

Learn to Pray Spontaneously as the Spirit Prompts You.

Hear what D. Martyn Lloyd-Jones says about this matter:

> Always respond to every impulse to pray. The impulse to pray may come when you are reading or when you are battling with a text. I would make an absolute law of this–always obey such an impulse. Where does it come from? It is the work of the Holy Spirit; it is a part of the meaning of "Work out your own salvation with fear and trembling. For it is God which worketh in you both to will and to do of his good pleasure" (Phil. 2:12, 13). This often leads to some of the most remarkable experiences in the life of the minister. So never

resist, never postpone it, never push it aside because you are busy. Give yourself to it, yield to it.[17]

From this point on, begin your meetings with your mentor by reporting on your progress in becoming a disciplined, effective prayer warrior and Bible reader. Have your mentor hold you accountable for your progress in Bible reading and prayer.

15. Read, then meditate on Luke 10:38-42.

  a. How does this passage apply to you as a future shepherd among God's people?

  I am more involved c my practice, concerned c it on a regular basis than I am c having time to listen to God through his Word.
  Need to read, meditate, pray more

  b. What is the *"one thing"* Mary chose, "the good part, which shall not be taken away from her" (v. 42)? *she sat at Jesus's feet listening (quiet)*
  Martha was distracted by life

SCRIPTURE MEMORY ASSIGNMENT:

"When they had appointed elders for them in every church, having prayed with fasting, they commended them to the Lord in whom they had believed."   Acts 14:23

"'Be on guard for yourselves and for all the flock, among which the Holy Spirit has made you overseers, to shepherd the church of God which He purchased with His own blood.'"   Acts 20:28

[1] John Stott, *You Can Trust The Bible: Our Foundation for Belief and Obedience* (Grand Rapids: Discovery House, 1982), pp. 9, 10.

[2] S. Lewis Johnson, "From Knowledge to Life Through Christ: Colossians 1:9-14," audio cassette (Dallas: Believers' Chapel, 1968).

[3] Geoffrey Thomas, *Reading the Bible* (Edinburgh: The Banner of Truth Trust, 1980), p. 11.

[4] Ibid., p. 13.

[5] Ibid.

[6] *The Westminster Confession of Faith*, I, 9.

[7] Edward J. Carnell, *The Case for Orthodox Theology* (Philadelphia: Westminster Press, 1959), pp. 51-65.

[8] R. C. Sproul, *Knowing Scripture* (Downers Grove: InterVarsity, 1977).

[9] Donald Whitney, *Spiritual Disciplines for the Christian Life* (Colorado Springs: NavPress, 1991), p. 77.

[10] Ibid., p. 62.

[11] D. A. Carson, *A Call to Spiritual Reformation* (Grand Rapids: Baker, 1992), p. 9.

[12] Andrew Murray, *With Christ in the School of Prayer* (1835; New York: Revell, n.d.), p. 6.

[13] D. Martyn Lloyd-Jones, *Studies in the Sermon on the Mount,* 2 vols. (Grand Rapids: Eerdmans, 1971), 2: 46.

[14] Whitney, *Spiritual Disciplines for the Christian Life*, p. 72.

[15] Roger Steer, *Spiritual Secrets of George Müller* (Wheaton: Harold Shaw, 1985), pp. 62, 63.

[16] John Piper, *Desiring God: Meditations of a Christian Hedonist* (Portland: Multnomah, 1986), pp. 150, 151.

[17] D. Martyn Lloyd-Jones, *The Preacher and Preaching* (Grand Rapids: Zondervan, 1971), p. 395.

LESSON 4

PROTECTING THE FLOCK FROM FALSE TEACHERS
THE SOURCE OF THE ELDERS' STRENGTH
THE PAULINE MODEL FOR ELDERS

LESSON OVERVIEW

Lesson 4 deals with the elders' solemn duty to protect their flock from "savage wolves," that is, false teachers. It covers Paul's farewell message to the Ephesian elders in Acts 20:18-35. An elder who desires to be a faithful guardian of Christ's Word and flock must become thoroughly familiar with this Scripture passage. It answers the question of who places elders in the local church as overseers and pastor shepherds, and establishes the inestimable worth of the body of Christ, which elders are called to guard from Satanic workers.

The second half of the lesson addresses the elders' need to trust in God and His Word for strength and guidance. It also explores Paul's example of self-employment and generosity to others.

PROTECTING THE FLOCK FROM FALSE TEACHERS

"'Be on guard for yourselves and for all the flock, among which the Holy Spirit has made you overseers, to shepherd the church of God which He purchased with His own blood. I know that after my departure savage wolves will come in among you, not sparing the flock; and from among your own selves men will arise, speaking perverse things, to draw away the disciples after them. Therefore be on the alert, remembering that night and day for a period of three years I did not cease to admonish each one with tears.'"

Acts 20:28-31

> Review pages 17-22, 27-29, 31-34, 109-115, 140-147. Read pages 147-159.

1. According to *Biblical Eldership* (pp. 19, 20), major failures on the part of local church leaders (shepherd elders) during the last century caused leading denominations and churches to abandon historic, biblical Christianity. What were these failures?

   Failed to keep watch
   Failed to be alert
   leaders were naive, untaught, prayerless
   preoccupied with self interests & self comforts

a.

b.

c.

2. In the context of Acts 20:28-31, what does the Greek verb *proseçhō* mean? (See p. 145.)

to keep watch – pay strict attention – continuous action

3. The essence of Paul's final message to the Ephesian elders is: ***Guard the church, wolves are coming.*** Since protecting the church against false teachers is one of the elders' major duties, what qualifications are especially necessary and why?

1 Timothy 3:2-7

1. Above reproach
2. The husband of one wife
3. Temperate [self-controlled, balanced]
4. Prudent [sensible, good judgment]
5. Respectable [well-behaved, virtuous]
6. Hospitable
7. Able to teach
8. Not addicted to wine
9. Not pugnacious [not belligerent]
10. Gentle [forbearing]
11. Peaceable [uncontentious]
12. Free from the love of money
13. Manages his household well
14. Not a new convert
15. A good reputation with those outside the church

Titus 1:6-9

1. Above reproach
2. The husband of one wife
3. Having children who believe
4. Not self-willed
5. Not quick-tempered
6. Not addicted to wine
7. Not pugnacious
8. Not fond of sordid gain
9. Hospitable
10. Lover of what is good [kind, virtuous]
11. Sensible [see prudent]
12. Just [righteous conduct, law-abiding]
13. Devout [holy, pleasing to God, loyal to His Word]
14. Self-controlled
15. Holds fast the faithful [trustworthy NIV] Word, both to exhort and to refute

1 Peter 5:1-3

1. Not shepherding under compulsion, but voluntarily
2. Not shepherding for sordid gain, but with eagerness
3. Not lording it over the flock, but proving to be an example

a. Able to teach

b. lover of what is good

c. devout (holy, pleasing to God)

d. self-controlled

e. holds fast the faithful Word of God - exhorts / refutes

4. What does the little word "all" in verse 28 teach about the work of the eldership?

   all the flock - not just the one's we are comfortable with

5. As a shepherd, you must know the condition and needs of the sheep you are responsible to guard. Jesus said that He knew His sheep and they knew His voice (John 10:2, 27). The spiritual care of the flock of God requires earnest prayer on the part of the shepherds for the sheep. Some have found it profitable to pray for two or three families in the congregation each day. Another way elders can begin to know the people more intimately is to visit each member's home and invite members into their homes.

   a. Discuss the above ideas. Do you have other suggestions or plans for getting to know the people?

      - Begin praying for my list - Fridge /office (post-it)
      - Have people over

   b. If the ratio of members to elders in your church is too large to permit individual attention by the elders, how do you propose the need to know the people be dealt with, so that the elders fulfill the scriptural mandates?

6. Why is it better to translate the Greek word *episkopos* as "overseer" rather than as "bishop"? What does the Greek term *episkopos* teach you about the work of an elder?

    a.

    b.

7. List several ways in which the knowledge that the Holy Spirit of God sovereignly placed you in the local church as an overseer should impact your work and thinking.

    a.

    b.

    c.

> "'Shepherd the church of God, which he bought with the blood of his Own' (20:28). With this we touch the mainspring of all true defense and shepherding of the church: the cost at which God bought it. That cost was the blood of his own, that is, of his own dear, loved, cherished Son. The story still has power to stagger imagination." David Gooding[1]

8. Discouragement is a leading reason why many shepherd elders leave the work. Endless problems, battles, and criticisms cause every elder to question, at one time or another, *Is it worth all this frustration and stress?* When you experience discouragement and want to give up, remember Paul's words to the elders in Acts 20:28: "Shepherd the church of God which He purchased with His own blood."

    a. What basic, fundamental Christian doctrines are expressed by the clause, "which He purchased with His own blood"?

- if God has given his very life for us, we should out of love & self-sacrifice continue to serve as long as we feel God has called us.

b. When you are discouraged and tempted to quit, how do the words, "the church of God which He purchased with His own blood," encourage you to persevere in your shepherding work?

God gave his own life

c. How do the words, "the church of God which He purchased with His own blood," affect your thinking about the work of protecting the church from false doctrine?

if he gave his blood for the church, we need to defend the truth for which he died.

9. What do the following images teach you about the nature and people of "the church of God," which you are called by the Holy Spirit to protect from false teachers?

a. **"The bride,"** Rev. 21:9

the "wife of the Lamb" — the church of God is the wife, the true love for whom he died & became the sacrificial lamb.

b. **"The household of God,"** 1 Tim. 3:15

the church is the household or family of God

10. What does Paul's example in Acts 20 teach about how you should guard your flock?

Acts 20:18, 19 *Paul served the Lord "with great humility & tears" he truly cared for the flock, the household, the bride of Christ*

LESSON 4

Acts 20:20, 21

Acts 20:26, 27

Acts 20:31

Acts 20:33-35

11.   Elders have been given a divine mandate to guard the flock of God from false teachers. Thus, shepherds must know as much as possible about the crafty ways of their archenemies. During the past two thousand years of Christian history, false teachers have been enormously successful in ravishing churches and denominations.

     Just as Satan does not call attention to himself, false teachers do not advertise their purpose. Initially they are hard to identify. In order to increase your ability to be a discerning elder, study the following passages. Using commentaries, list the characteristics of the false teacher.

    a.   The **evil motives** of the false teacher:

       Matt. 23:6-12; Gal. 6:12

       Phil. 3:18, 19; 1 Tim. 6:5; Titus 1:11

       1 Tim. 4:1-3

b. The **subtlety** of the false teacher:

2 Tim. 3:13

c. The **disguises** of the false teacher:

Matt. 7:15; 24:24; 2 Cor. 11:13-15

d. The **distinguishing marks** of the false teacher concerning:

Morality:

Jer. 23:14

2 Tim. 3:6

2 Peter 2:2, 10 , 14, 18, 19

Jude 4, 18, 19

Truth:

Jer. 23:14

2 Tim. 3:8, 13

2 Peter 2: 2, 18

Jude 18

1 Tim. 4:2

Titus 1:10

Authority:

Jude 8, 19

2 Peter 2:10

Titus 1:10

e.   The **teachings** of the false teacher:

Col. 2:4, 8, 18, 19

1 Tim. 6:3-5

Gal. 1:9; 1 Tim. 4:1-3; 2 Peter 2:1;
2 John 7

Deut. 13:1-3, 5, 6; Jer. 23:25, 26,
28, 30-32; Col. 2:18

f.   The **deeds** of the false teacher:

Jer. 10:21; 23:1, 2; Acts 20:29, 30

Rom. 16:17, 18; Gal. 1:6, 7;
1 Tim. 1:3-7; 6:3-5; Titus 3:10, 11;
Jude 19

12.   As a church leader, you must clearly recognize and persistently confront the false teacher's methods. According to *Biblical Eldership* (pp. 31-34), what key method does the false teacher consistently use to spread and maintain false doctrines?

13.   Describe the false teacher (as studied above) who would pose the greatest threat to your congregation. Explain why such a person would be a great threat.

a.

b.

14. What contemporary false doctrines (secular or religious) may possibly invade your church in the near future? What are you doing by way of study and teaching to protect your flock and defend the truth of the Word from these errors?

a. Examples:

b. Preparation:

Counterfeits in the Church

"What comes to mind when you hear the terms 'false prophets' and 'false teachers'? Many people tend to think of Eastern mystics and gurus, the spokespersons for nonbiblical religions, or dynamic cult leaders–people who are recognizably outside the boundaries of the Christian church. But the apostle Peter devoted an entire chapter in one of his letters to false prophets and teachers who operate within the church: 'But false prophets also arose among the people, just as there will be false teachers among you, who will secretly introduce destructive heresies, even denying the Master who bought them, bringing swift destruction upon themselves' (2 Peter 2:1). These people are in our churches right now, disguised as workers of righteousness.

"Notice that the lure of false teachers is not primarily their doctrine: 'And many will follow their sensuality, and because of them the way of the truth will be maligned' (v. 2). What does Peter mean by 'follow their sensuality'? He is talking about Christians who evaluate a ministry based on the outward appearance and charm of its leaders. We say, 'He's such a nice guy'; 'She's a very charismatic person'; 'He's a real dynamic speaker'? 'She's so sweet and sounds so sincere.' But is physical attractiveness a biblical criterion for validating a ministry or a teacher? Of course not! The issue is always truth and righteousness, and false teachers who appeal to the physical senses have maligned the way of the truth.

"Peter goes on to reveal two ways by which we can identify false prophets and false teachers who operate within the church. First, they will be involved in immorality of some kind, indulging 'the flesh in its corrupt desires' (v. 10). They may be discovered in illicit activities involving sex and/or money. They may be antinomian, claiming that God is all love and grace so we don't need to abide by any law. Their immorality may not be easy to spot, but it will eventually surface in their lives (2 Corinthians 11:15).

False prophets

"Second, false prophets and teachers 'despise authority' and are 'daring, self-willed' (2 Peter 2:10). These people have an independent spirit. They do their own thing and won't answer to anybody. They either won't submit to the authority of a denomination or board, or they will pick their own board which will simply rubber-stamp anything they want to do.

"There are historic leadership roles in Scripture: prophet (preaching and teaching), priest (pastoring and shepherding), and king (administration). Only Jesus in His perfection is capable of occupying all three roles simultaneously. I believe we need the checks and balances of a plurality of elders in the church, distributing the three critical roles to more than one person. No one can survive his own unchallenged authority. Every true, committed Christian in a leadership role needs to submit himself and his ideas to other mature believers who will hold him accountable."

Neil Anderson[2]

THE SOURCE OF THE ELDERS' STRENGTH

"'And now I commend you to God and to the word of His grace, which is able to build you up and to give you the inheritance among all those who are sanctified. . . .' When he had said these things, he knelt down and prayed with them all. And they began to weep aloud and embraced Paul, and repeatedly kissed him, grieving especially over the word which he had spoken, that they would see his face no more. And they were accompanying him to the ship."

Acts 20:32, 36-38

Review pages 153-159.

15.   As Paul departed from Asia Minor, he entrusted the church elders to God and the Word of God. As spiritual leaders bereft of their founding father and mentor, the elders were to trust solely in God and the Word of God for help, strength, guidance, blessing, and wisdom. They were, therefore, to be models of faith in God and in the Word of God. Trusting God is not only absolutely fundamental to salvation but also to living for Christ (Gal. 2:20). As the Scripture says, "Man does not live by bread alone, but man lives by everything that proceeds out of the mouth of the Lord" (Deut. 8:3b).

Elders who do not trust in God and His Word have nothing more than their own feeble strength and wisdom to draw upon for help, and they inevitably mislead the flock of God into a desert of deadly false teachings. As a future pastor elder, what do each of the following Scripture texts teach you about faith, that is, *trust,* in God and His Word?

Jer. 17:5, 7 Thus says the Lord, "Cursed is the man who trusts in mankind and makes flesh his strength, and whose heart turns away from the Lord. . . . Blessed is the man who trusts in the Lord and whose trust is the Lord."

Don't trust your own strength → cursed
Trust God   → blessed

Isa. 31:1 Woe to those who go down to Egypt for help and rely on horses, and trust in chariots because they are many and in horsemen because they are very strong, but they do not look to the Holy One of Israel, nor seek the Lord!

Isa. 66:2*b* "But to this one I will look, to him who is humble and contrite of spirit, and who trembles at My word."

Ps. 56:3, 4 When I am afraid, I will put my trust in You. In God, whose word I praise, in God I have put my trust; I shall not be afraid. What can mere man do to me?

— Megan

Prov. 3:5-7 Trust in the Lord with all your heart and do not lean on your own understanding. In all your ways acknowledge Him, and He will make your paths straight. Do not be wise in your own eyes; fear the Lord and turn away from evil.

Matt. 6:30-33 "'But if God so clothes the grass of the field, which is alive today and tomorrow is thrown into the furnace, will He not much more clothe you? You of little faith! Do not worry then, saying, "What will we eat?" or "What will we drink?" or "What will we wear for clothing?" For the Gentiles eagerly seek all these things; for your heavenly Father knows that you need all these things. But seek first His kingdom and His righteousness, and all these things will be added to you.'"

Megan

Heb. 10:35, 36, 38-11:2, 6 Therefore, do not throw away your confidence, which has a great reward. For you have need of endurance, so that when you have done the will of God, you may receive what was promised. . . . But My righteous one shall live by faith; and if he shrinks back, My soul has no pleasure in him. But we are not of those who shrink back to destruction, but of those who have faith to the preserving of the soul. Now faith is the assurance of things hoped for, the conviction of things not seen. For by it the men of old gained approval. . . . And without faith it is impossible to please Him, for he who comes to God must believe that He is and that He is a rewarder of those who seek Him.

God has no pleasure in the one who shrinks back —
the righteous live by faith
without faith, it is impossible to please God
God is a rewarder of those who seek Him

2 Cor. 1:8, 9 For we do not want you to be unaware, brethren, of our affliction which came to us in Asia, that we were burdened excessively, beyond our strength, so that we despaired even of life; indeed, we had the sentence of death within ourselves so that we would not trust in ourselves, but in God who raises the dead.

Gal. 2:20 "'I have been crucified with Christ; and it is no longer I who live, but Christ lives in me; and the life which I now live in the flesh I live by faith in the Son of God, who loved me and gave Himself up for me.'"

Eph. 6:13, 16 Therefore, take up the full armor of God, so that you will be able to resist in the evil day, and having done everything, to stand firm. . . . In addition to all, taking up the shield of faith with which you will be able to extinguish all the flaming arrows of the evil one.

In addition/Above all take the shield of faith

THE PAULINE MODEL FOR ELDERS

"'I have coveted no one's silver or gold or clothes. You yourselves know that these hands ministered to my own needs and to the men who were with me. In everything I showed you that by working hard in this manner you must help the weak and remember the words of the Lord Jesus, that He Himself said, "It is more blessed to give than to receive."'"

Acts 20:33-35

Review pages 144-159.

16. Paul set a personal example of earning his own living while planting and shepherding the churches, a practice we now refer to as *tentmaking*. In 2 Thessalonians 3:7-11, 1 Corinthians 9:14-19, and 2 Corinthians 11:8-12, 30, Paul further comments on his practice.

a. What were Paul's reasons for tentmaking?

- To be busy working - to eat, you must work
- the gospel should be free to all -
- Kept him from being a financial burden

b. How do we reconcile Paul's personal example with 1 Cor. 9:14?

- those who preach should receive their living from the gospel
- fully devoted vs. part-time focus

c. Why do you think churches give less honor to those who support themselves while at the same time ministering to the church than to those who are supported by the church and thus are deemed to be "in full-time service"?

17. What does the fact that the first churches were shepherded–that is pastored–by ordinary men, who earned their own bread, reveal about Christian ministry? (See heading, "Hard Work," pp. 27-29, and pp. 109-115; cf. lesson 5, question **10.**)

a. Their devotion/passion led them to work hard

b. we need to encourage/rely on all the church to participate. "no free rides" - people need to diversify the work load

c.

SCRIPTURE MEMORY ASSIGNMENT:

"'I know that after my departure savage wolves will come in among you, not sparing the flock; and from among your own selves men will arise, speaking perverse things, to draw away the disciples after them. Therefore be on the alert, remembering that night and day for a period of three years I did not cease to admonish each one with tears. And now I commend you to God and to the word of His grace, which is able to build you up and to give you the inheritance among all those who are sanctified. I have coveted no one's silver or gold or clothes. You yourselves know that these hands ministered to my own needs and to the men who were with me. In everything I showed you that by working hard in this manner you must help the weak and remember the words of the Lord Jesus, that He Himself said, "It is more blessed to give than to receive."'"

Acts 20:29-35

---

[1] David Gooding, *True to the Faith: A Fresh Approach to the Acts of the Apostles* (London: Hodder & Stoughton, 1990), p. 360.

[2] Neil Anderson, *The Bondage Breaker* (Eugene: Harvest House, 1990), pp. 163, 164.

LESSON 5

HUMBLE SERVANTS AND THE CHIEF SHEPHERD
HARD-WORKING MEN

LESSON OVERVIEW

Lesson 5 covers 1 Peter 5:1*a*, 3*b*-5 and 1 Thessalonians 5:12, 13. Peter exhorts elders to shepherd the flock through the power of personal example and encourages them with the promises of the glorious return of the "Chief Shepherd" and the "crown of glory." Finally, he calls elders, as well as the flock, to clothe themselves with humility so that all may live together in peace.

Paul's exhortation to the congregation at Thessalonica reinforces the elders' task of leading and admonishing the congregation. In order to bear this great responsibility, pastor elders must be self-disciplined, highly committed disciples of the Master. Clearly, board elders cannot pastor a local church: only hard-working, self-disciplined, shepherd elders can.

Like Peter, Paul also calls the congregation and its leaders to work for peace and to love one another. Without humility, love, and peace there is little hope of experiencing the joys of Christlike community and effective pastoral leadership.

HUMBLE SERVANTS AND THE CHIEF SHEPHERD

"**Therefore, I exhort the elders among you, . . . be examples to the flock. And when the Chief Shepherd appears, you will receive the unfading crown of glory. You younger men, likewise, be subject to your elders; and all of you, clothe yourselves with humility toward one another, for God is opposed to the proud, but gives grace to the humble.**"   1 Peter 5:1*a*, 3*b*-5

Read pages 249-252.

1. Why is a leader's personal example of godly character and conduct absolutely necessary to effective, long-term leadership within the local Christian church? (See also pp. 70-72, 78, 79.)

to model Christ's example as the Chief Shepherd

> "Sherwood Eddy, a missionary statesman and author, who knew [Amy Carmichael] well, was deeply impressed by the 'beauty of her character'; and character, according to Eddy, was the key to successful world evangelism. 'Here is the point where many a missionary breaks down. Every normal missionary sails with high purpose but as a very imperfect Christian . . . . His character is his weakest point . . . . It was just here that Miss Carmichael was a blessing to all who came into intimate and understanding contact with her radiant life . . . . Amy Wilson Carmichael was the most Christlike character I ever met, and . . . her life was the most fragrant, the most joyfully sacrificial, that I ever knew.'"
>
> Ruth A. Tucker[1]

2.   In his book *Spiritual Leadership*, J. Oswald Sanders writes, "Leadership is influence, the ability of one person to influence others."[2] Ask your wife or a close friend to help you answer the following questions.

   a.   Which traits in your spiritual life and service will make your leadership influential in the flock?

   b.   Which traits may have an adverse effect on your leadership influence?

3.   Why was the promise of the Chief Shepherd's appearance significant to the Asian elders?

4. Evaluate the effect that your awareness of the Chief Shepherd's imminent return and His reward for faithful service has on your ministry. Choose the two statements below that best represent your thinking, and explain why you hold each view.

    __ I believe the doctrines, but they have little effect on my thinking.
    __ I rarely think about these matters.
    __ I have no idea what these promises mean.
    ✓ I often think of His evaluation of my work when He returns; this motivates me to better service.
    ✓ I am encouraged and comforted by the thought of His appearance; it keeps me going in the face of discouragement and setbacks.
    __ My work as an elder is unaffected by the thought of future reward.
    __ I am looking forward to the day of reward in the presence of Christ my Lord.

5. Peter exhorts both the young men and elders of the churches of northwestern Asia Minor to "clothe yourselves with humility." Humility is central to the spirit of the Christian community, especially to the church eldership team. Write out a short definition of humility. It will be helpful to check both secular and theological dictionaries.

6. The virtue of humility is absolutely indispensable for a team of elders who are called to work together in unity and peace. Summarize seven principles that explain why humility is essential. The following passages (as well as chapter 5, pp. 85-98) will help.

Obad. 3 "The arrogance of your heart has deceived you, you who live in the clefts of the rock, in the loftiness of your dwelling place, who say in your heart, 'Who will bring me down to earth?'"

Arrogance → deceives

2 Chron. 26:3a, 16 Uzziah was sixteen years old when he became king, and he reigned fifty-two years in Jerusalem. . . . But when he became strong, his heart was so proud that he acted corruptly, and he was unfaithful to the Lord his God, for he entered the temple of the Lord to burn incense on the altar of incense.

pride → corruption, unfaithfulness

2 Chron. 32:24-26 In those days Hezekiah became mortally ill; and he prayed to the Lord, and the Lord spoke to him and gave him a sign. But Hezekiah gave no return for the benefit he received, because his heart was proud; therefore wrath came on him and on Judah and Jerusalem. However, Hezekiah humbled the pride of his heart, both he and the inhabitants of Jerusalem, so that the wrath of the Lord did not come on them in the days of Hezekiah.

Pride → God's wrath

Prov. 11:2b With the humble is wisdom.

Humble → wisdom

Prov. 13:10 Through presumption [insolence] comes nothing but strife, but with those who receive counsel is wisdom. *humble/counsel ⇒ wisdom*

Prov. 16:18 Pride goes before destruction, and a haughty spirit before stumbling.

Prov. 26:12 Do you see a man wise in his own eyes? There is more hope for a fool than for him. *pride → more hope for a fool*

Isa. 66:2 "For My hand made all these things, thus all these things came into being," declares the Lord. "But to this one I will look, to him who is humble and contrite of spirit, and who trembles at My word." *humbleness, contrite spirit, trembles/awe of God's Word = God looks to this person*

Luke 14:10, 11 "But when you are invited, go and recline at the last place, so that when the one who has invited you comes, he may say to you, 'Friend, move up higher'; then you will have honor in the sight of all who are at the table with you. For everyone who exalts himself will be humbled, and he who humbles himself will be exalted."

Eph. 4:1, 2 Therefore I, the prisoner of the Lord, implore you to walk in a manner worthy of the calling with which you have been called, with all humility and gentleness, with patience, showing tolerance [forbearance] for one another in love. *live w humility, gentleness, patience, be tolerant*

Phil. 2:3-5 Do nothing from selfishness or empty conceit, but with humility of mind regard one another as more important than yourselves; do not merely look out for your own personal interests, but also for the interests of others. Have this attitude in yourselves which was also in Christ Jesus. *Christ's attitude = others more important*

Col. 3:12 So, as those who have been chosen of God, holy and beloved, put on a heart of compassion, kindness, humility, gentleness and patience.

a. *see above note*

b.

c.

e.

f.

g.

The admonition to be a peacemaker is sometimes misunderstood as meaning that we are to humbly maintain the peace. Peacemaking, however, does not mean that problems are not confronted. Rather, they are addressed in such a way, with humility and gentleness, that the outcome is peace within the congregation. In 2 Thessalonians 3:14-16, for example, Paul urges decisive action that will ultimately restore peace. The passive overlooking of sin for the purpose of maintaining peace is never taught in Scripture.

HARD-WORKING MEN

"But we request of you, brethren, that you appreciate those who diligently labor among you, and have charge over [Greek, *prohistēmi*] you in the Lord and give you instruction [admonish NIV; Greek, *noutheteo*], and that you esteem them very highly in love because of their work. Live in peace with one another."   I Thessalonians 5:12, 13

Read pages 161-174.

7. In his letters to the churches, why did Paul *not* call on the elders (or any other leaders) to handle problems or difficulties within the church (see also pp. 291-295)? How does this fact affect your thinking toward the congregation and your leadership over the congregation?

    a.

    b.

    c.

    d.

8. What is meant by the statement on p. 27 of *Biblical Eldership*: "Biblical eldership, however, cannot exist in an atmosphere of nominal Christianity"? Review pp. 27-29.

True Biblical elders need to have diligence & focus to obey & be absorbed in God's Word - it is not a passive position

9. How does Luke 14:25-33 apply to a prospective elder?

— Our love for Christ should be so strong that our love for family & friends should appear as hatred

— Carry our cross & follow Christ. / Estimate the cost of being a Biblical elder

---

"I defy you to read the life of any saint that has ever adorned the life of the Church without seeing at once that the greatest characteristic in the life of that saint was discipline and order. Invariably it is the universal characteristic of all the outstanding men and women of God . . . . Obviously it is something that is thoroughly scriptural and absolutely essential."

D. Martyn Lloyd-Jones[3]

"It has been well said that the future is with the disciplined and that quality has been placed first on our list, for without it the other gifts, however great, will never realize their maximum potential. Only the disciplined person will rise to his highest powers. He is able to lead because he has conquered himself."

J. Oswald Sanders[4]

Building a house / going to war — never 3 estimating the cost

10. As our text states, elders *work hard* at leading and admonishing the church. Elders must be disciplined men who keep their priorities straight and wisely manage their time and responsibilities. What do the following Scripture texts teach about the necessity of self-discipline in a spiritual leader's life?

Gal. 5:22*a*, 23*a* But the fruit of the Spirit is love, joy, . . . self-control.

Titus 1:7*a*, 8 For the overseer must be above reproach as God's steward, . . . hospitable, loving what is good, sensible, just, devout, self-controlled [disciplined].

1 Tim. 4:7b Discipline yourself for the purpose of godliness.

1 Cor. 9:25-27 Everyone who competes in the games exercises self-control in all things. They then do it to receive a perishable wreath, but we an imperishable. Therefore I run in such a way, as not without aim; I box in such a way, as not beating the air; but I beat [discipline] my body and make it my slave, so that, after I have preached to others, I myself will not be disqualified.

Prov. 25:28 Like a city that is broken into and without walls is a man who has no control over his spirit.

Prov. 16:32 He who is slow to anger is better than the mighty, and he who rules his spirit, than he who captures a city.

11. Of the following elder qualifications, choose those that relate to self-discipline and explain how they apply.

1 Timothy 3:2-7	**Titus 1:6-9**	**1 Peter 5:1-3**
1. Above reproach	1. Above reproach	1. Not shepherding under compulsion, but voluntarily
2. The husband of one wife _[not into lust, flirting, pornography]_	2. The husband of one wife	2. Not shepherding for sordid gain, but with eagerness
3. Temperate [self-controlled, balanced]	3. Having children who believe	3. Not lording it over the flock, but proving to be an example
4. Prudent [sensible, good judgment]	4. Not self-willed	
5. Respectable [well-behaved, virtuous]	5. Not quick-tempered	
6. Hospitable	6. Not addicted to wine _–disciplined c drinking_	
7. Able to teach— _learn 1st / take the time_	7. Not pugnacious	
8. Not addicted to wine	8. Not fond of sordid gain	
9. Not pugnacious [not belligerent]	9. Hospitable	
10. Gentle [forbearing]	10. Lover of what is good [kind, virtuous]	
11. Peaceable [uncontentious]	11. Sensible [see prudent]	
12. Free from the love of money _disciplined c money_	12. Just [righteous conduct, law-abiding] _– Knowing what is just –learning_	
13. Manages his household well _↳ discipline children_	13. Devout [holy, pleasing to God, loyal to His Word]	
14. Not a new convert	14. Self-controlled	
15. A good reputation with those outside the church	15. Holds fast the faithful [trustworthy NIV] Word, both to exhort and to refute	

a.

b.

c.

d.

e.

f.

12. Read the quote by R. Paul Stevens on pp. 28, 29. What does Stevens mean by his statement that "tentmakers must live a pruned life and literally find leisure and rest in the rhythm of serving Christ" (Matt. 11:28)?

*We have to be willing to find our leisure, fun, rest, in/thru the church, while serving – while working

Develop leisure/rest c̄ those we are called to serve

13. To be effective as a shepherd elder, you must clearly understand the elders' identity and function in the church. Define the Greek term *prohistēmi*. How does this term clarify the position and work of the elders (see pp. 167, 168)?

a. Ruling

while

b. Providing care

at home first c̄ our household second → then our elder role should mimic our household abilities of ruling while providing care

14. To gain an accurate picture of the elders' work, you must also understand the meaning of the Greek term *noutheteo̅*.

    a. What does *noutheteo̅* entail?

    b. Why is the ministry of admonition vitally important to a Christian congregation (see pp. 151-153, 165-169)?

15. A shepherd must be very concerned about the peace of the flock, and it should weigh heavily in all the elders' discussions or decisions. From the above lists of elder qualifications, which qualifications relate to peacemaking? Explain the role each plays.

    a.

    b.

    c.

    d.

    e.

16. Among the qualifications you have just listed, *gentle* stands out for making peace amidst disagreement and failure.

    a. Define this excellent character quality.

b. Explain how gentleness establishes peace among the Lord's people.

> "Self-sacrificing love is thus made the essence of the self-sacrificing love of Christ himself: Christ's followers are to 'have the same mind in them which was also in Christ Jesus.' The possessive pronouns throughout this passage [John 15]–'abide in *my* love,' 'in *my* love,' 'in *his* (the Father's) love'–are all subjective: so that throughout the whole, it is the love which Christ bears his people which is kept in prominent view as the impulse and standard of the love he asks."
> B. B. Warfield[5]

17. Paul E. Billheimer says the local church is a "laboratory" of love (p. 171).[6] If this is so, explain how serving on the eldership team would be a far greater testing ground of love?

SCRIPTURE MEMORY ASSIGNMENT:

"But we request of you, brethren, that you appreciate those who diligently labor among you, and have charge over you in the Lord and give you instruction, and that you esteem them very highly in love because of their work. Live in peace with one another." 1 Thessalonians 5:12, 13

---

[1] Ruth A. Tucker, *From Jerusalem to Irian Jaya: A Biographical History of Christian Missions* (Grand Rapids: Zondervan, 1983), p. 239.

[2] J. Oswald Sanders, *Spiritual Leadership* (Chicago: Moody, 1967, 1980), p. 35.

[3] D. Martyn Lloyd-Jones, *Spiritual Depression* (Grand Rapids: Eerdmans, 1965), p. 210.

[4] Sanders, *Spiritual Leadership,* p. 67.

[5] B. B. Warfield, "The Emotional Life of Our Lord," in *The Person and Work of Christ* (Philadelphia: Presbyterian and Reformed, 1950), p. 104.

[6] Paul E. Billheimer, *Love Covers* (Fort Washington: Christian Literature Crusade, 1981), p. 34.

LESSON 6

TEAM LEADERSHIP

LESSON OVERVIEW

Lesson 6 examines the plurality of overseers mentioned in Philippians 1:1, the equating of overseers with elders, the significance of church leadership terminology, the importance and practice of team leadership, and the principle of "first among equals."

The major focus of the lesson is on learning how to work with fellow elders in Christian harmony, which is not an easy task. Becoming a good team player takes years of effort and commitment. The key to team leadership is *agapē* love.

ELDER: THE OFFICE AND THE TITLE

"Paul and Timothy, bond-servants of Christ Jesus, to all the saints in Christ Jesus who are in Philippi, including the overseers and deacons."
Philippians 1:1

Review pages 31-34. Read pages 174-180.
---

1. According to *Biblical Eldership*, "Paul's brief mention of overseers and deacons provides a wealth of valuable information for our study on eldership" (p. 174). What special contributions to our understanding of the New Testament concept of eldership are made by Philippians 1:1?

a. balance oversight

b.

    c.

2. What biblical evidence do we have to prove the assertion that the "overseers" mentioned in Philippians 1:1 are the same group of leaders who are called ***elders*** elsewhere? List the biblical arguments equating "overseers" with elders, in order of decreasing significance for you.

    a.

    b.

    c.

    d.

3. Why should the terminology (or titles) we use to describe our church leaders be a matter of critical importance to the local church?

    a.

    b.

4. What titles does your church use for its leaders? In what ways do these accurately represent (or misrepresent) the language and concepts of the New Testament church?

ASSIGNMENT:

In Philippians 1:1, deacons are closely associated with elders (overseers). To help you know who deacons are and what they do, consider reading *Ministers of Mercy: The New Testament Deacon.*[1] It would also be profitable to observe the deacons at work in your church.

PLURALITY OF ELDERS AND OVERSEERS

Review pages 35-45, 101-117.

5. According to *Biblical Eldership* (p. 35), "The New Testament provides *conclusive evidence* that the pastoral oversight of the apostolic churches was a team effort–not the sole responsibility of one person." What evidence does *Biblical Eldership* present to justify this strong statement?

    a.   Balancing the oversight.

    b.   No "power" figure

    c.   "two heads" better than one

    d.   Sick to call for the "elders" (plural)

    e.   quoted "overseers" plural Phil. 1:1

    f.   James 5:15 plural

    g.   Acts 14:23

    h.

6. In what ways does church government by a plurality of elders preserve the true, biblical nature of the local church as designed by God?

    a.

    b.

    c.

    d.

7. One of the significant benefits of team leadership is that it provides genuine accountability for leaders (pp. 42-44). In what ways is mutual *accountability* both a practical benefit to the elders and an important theological reason for plurality of leadership?

    a.   Practical benefits:

    b.   Theological reason:

8. How would you answer those who say that James was the senior pastor of the church in Jerusalem (pp. 104-106)?

9. From the elder qualification lists below, which character traits are necessary for working in close Christian harmony with others on the eldership team? List the characteristics in decreasing order of importance and explain why each is important.

1 Timothy 3:2-7	**Titus 1:6-9**	**1 Peter 5:1-3**
1. Above reproach	1. Above reproach	1. Not shepherding under compulsion, but voluntarily
2. The husband of one wife	2. The husband of one wife	2. Not shepherding for sordid gain, but with eagerness
3. Temperate [self-controlled, balanced]	3. Having children who believe	3. Not lording it over the flock, but proving to be an example
4. Prudent [sensible, good judgment]	4. Not self-willed	
5. Respectable [well-behaved, virtuous]	5. Not quick-tempered	
6. Hospitable	6. Not addicted to wine	
7. Able to teach	7. Not pugnacious	
8. Not addicted to wine	8. Not fond of sordid gain	
9. Not pugnacious [not belligerent]	9. Hospitable	
10. Gentle [forbearing]	10. Lover of what is good [kind, virtuous]	
11. Peaceable [uncontentious]	11. Sensible [see prudent]	
12. Free from the love of money	12. Just [righteous conduct, law-abiding]	
13. Manages his household well	13. Devout [holy, pleasing to God, loyal to His Word]	
14. Not a new convert	14. Self-controlled	
15. A good reputation with those outside the church	15. Holds fast the faithful [trustworthy NIV] Word, both to exhort and to refute	

a.

b.

c.

d.

e.

f.

g.

10. From your past experience in working with committees or groups, indicate whether the following statements apply: use **T** for true, or **F** for false. Take time to honestly evaluate yourself before God. Ask your wife or a close friend to help you answer objectively.

_____ I act impulsively and dislike waiting for others to make decisions.

_____ I generally trust the collective judgment of my fellow team members.

_____ I feel genuine concern for the interests and plans of my fellow workers.

_____ I often act independently of the leadership body.

_____ I make myself accountable to my fellow team members.

_____ I work hard to cooperate with my partners in ministry.

_____ I share my burdens, fears, and problems with my brothers.

_____ I am inclined to carry a grudge.

_____ I am easily frustrated by disagreement.

_____ I am afraid to speak honestly in a group.

_____ I feel free to correct and direct my fellow team members.

_____ I actively contribute to discussions and decisions.

_____ I tend to be bossy.

_____ I am too sensitive.

_____ I tend to dominate discussions.

_____ I have a hard time apologizing or admitting I am wrong.

_____ I love my fellow colleagues.

_____ I consciously try to be humble and serve my brothers.

_____ I pray for my team members regularly.

With your mentor's help, identify your areas of weakness as a team member. Give these weaknesses special prayer attention and peer accountability. Together, focus on how the profound quotation by Paul E. Billheimer (_Biblical Eldership,_ p. 171) applies to you.

11. The secret to unity and cooperation among elders is _agapē_ love. Read the following verses and list the characteristics of _agapē_ love that enable elders to work together in unity and peace and to handle the many hurts and disagreements leaders regularly encounter.

John 13:1, 4, 5, 14 Now before the Feast of the Passover, Jesus knowing that His hour had come that He would depart out of this world to the Father, having loved His own who were in the world, He loved them to the end. . . . [He] got up from supper, and laid aside His garments; and taking a towel, He girded Himself. Then He poured water into the basin, and began to wash the disciples' feet and to wipe them with the towel with which He was girded. . . . "If I then, the Lord and the Teacher, washed your feet, you also ought to wash one another's feet."

Rom. 12:9*a* Let love be without hypocrisy. Abhor what is evil.

Rom. 12:10 Be devoted to one another in brotherly love; give preference to one another in honor.

Rom. 14:15 For if because of food your brother is hurt, you are no longer walking according to love. Do not destroy with your food him for whom Christ died.

1 Cor. 8:1 Now concerning things sacrificed to idols, we know that we all have knowledge. Knowledge makes arrogant, but love edifies.

1 Cor. 13:4 Love is patient [suffers long], love is kind and is not jealous; love does not brag and is not arrogant.

1 Cor. 13:5 [Love] does not act unbecomingly; it does not seek its own, is not provoked, does not take into account a wrong suffered.

1 Cor. 13:8 Love never fails; but if there are gifts of prophecy, they will be done away; if there are tongues, they will cease; if there is knowledge, it will be done away.

Eph. 4:2 With all humility and gentleness, with patience, showing tolerance [forbearance] for one another in love.

Philem. 8, 9 Therefore, though I have enough confidence in Christ to order you to do what is proper, yet for love's sake I rather appeal to you–since I am such a person as Paul, the aged, and now also a prisoner of Christ Jesus.

1 Peter 4:8 Above all, keep fervent in your love for one another, because love covers a multitude of sins.

1 John 3:16 We know love by this, that He laid down His life for us; and we ought to lay down our lives for the brethren.

12. Which biblical concept above is God encouraging you to nurture and adopt?

First Among a Council of Equals: Leaders Among Leaders

"The elders who rule well are to be considered worthy of double honor, especially those who work hard at preaching and teaching. For the Scripture says, 'You shall not muzzle the ox while he is threshing,' and 'The laborer is worthy of his wages.'"
1 Timothy 5:17, 18

Review pages 45-50.

13. List examples from Peter's life and ministry that demonstrate the principle of "first among equals."

   a.

   b.

   c.

   d.

14. Which traits characterize an elder who is first among his equals?

    a.

    b.

    c.

15. How does the principle of "first among equals" help protect and sharpen an exceptionally gifted teacher and/or leader?

    a.

    b.

    c.

16. What is wrong with calling one elder "pastor" and the other men "elders"?

    a.

    b.

    c.

17. Plurality of leadership has inherent risks that may lead to weaknesses and frustrations in team ministry. In parallel columns, describe the inherent risks of shared leadership and the corresponding remedies.

Inherent Risks	**Remedies**

SCRIPTURE MEMORY ASSIGNMENT:

"The elders who rule well are to be considered worthy of double honor, especially those who work hard at preaching and teaching. For the Scripture says, 'You shall not muzzle the ox while he is threshing,' and 'The laborer is worthy of his wages.'"   1 Timothy 5:17, 18

---

[1] Alexander Strauch, *Ministers of Mercy: The New Testament Deacon* (Littleton: Lewis and Roth, 1992).

LESSON 7

QUALIFIED LEADERS

LESSON OVERVIEW

The major emphasis of lesson 7 is the necessity of church elders being "above reproach." The lesson also reviews Paul's purpose in writing 1 Timothy, the Ephesian elders' failure to protect the church from false teaching, the faithful saying of 1 Timothy 3:1, and the qualifications for overseers.

THE BOOK OF FIRST TIMOTHY

"I am writing these things to you, hoping to come to you before long; but in case I am delayed, I write so that you will know how one ought to conduct himself in the household of God, which is the church of the living God, the pillar and support of the truth." 1 Timothy 3:14, 15

Read pages 181-186.

1. According to 1 Timothy 3:14, 15:

   a. What was Paul's purpose in writing 1 Timothy?

   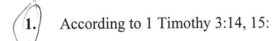 To teach conduct in God's house

   b. Why is eldership a vital part of that purpose?

   we are to exemplify & sustain the church of the living God, (the pillar & support of the church)

2. The church in Ephesus was thoroughly disrupted by false teachers who most likely came from within, just as Paul had predicted. *Biblical Eldership* suggests that the Ephesian elders made mistakes that you, as a future elder, can learn from and avoid repeating. What were these mistakes?

a. Women flaunting their wealth

b. Fighting between men - adversely affected their prayers

c. Needy widows were forsaken

d. Sin was ignored

e. the gospel message was therefore threatened.

ASSIGNMENTS:

Since "1 Timothy is the most important letter of the New Testament for the study of biblical eldership" (p. 181), you should own a number of sound commentaries on the Pastoral Epistles. We invest in any good commentary on the Pastoral Epistles.

You should also make use of expository preaching series on 1 Timothy and Titus.[1] Do not be limited to one favorite preacher. We can learn from all of God's servants, even those who are not part of our familiar circle (1 Cor. 3:21-23).

As soon as you are able, undertake an in-depth study of 1 Timothy and Titus. An excellent way to learn these books is to teach them to others, since you learn best when you teach.

A FAITHFUL SAYING

"It is a trustworthy statement: if any man aspires to the office of overseer, it is a fine work he desires to do. An overseer, then, must be above reproach."
1 Timothy 3:1, 2a

Review pages 186-188.

3.   Write out your own paraphrase of 1 Timothy 3:1. Be creative, using a number of sentences. For an example, see F. F. Bruce's paraphrase of Titus 1:5-7, on pp. 227, 228.

An authoritative truth: If any man aspires to be one of the overseers it is a good work
he must be trustworthy, the control of
he must be admirable, above sinful desires
above reproach

4.   To the best of your recollection:

a.   When did you first desire to be a shepherd elder?

~ 8 yrs ago - ?

b.   What sparked your initial desire to be a shepherd elder?

inner desire to help / teach others

c.   Describe an event or problem that has caused you to doubt your desire to be a shepherd elder.

personal challenges & marital challenges

d.   How intense is your desire to be a shepherd elder?

I feel it's a calling from God

e.   In what ways do you think an intense desire is appropriate or inappropriate?

to make sure its an intense desire based on <u>God's call</u>

f.   Do you ever doubt your qualifications to be an elder? If so, how seriously?

yes at times (see c)

g.   If, at this time, you are not appointed to be a shepherd elder, what should be your response?

Step down

5. Many people try to prove the senior pastor theory by the singular use of the word "overseer" in 1 Timothy 3:2 and Titus 1:7. How does *Biblical Eldership* explain the singular use of "overseer" in these two passages?

Overseer is a plural-used term

APOSTOLIC QUALIFICATIONS FOR ELDERSHIP

"An overseer, then, must be above reproach, the husband of one wife, temperate, prudent, respectable, hospitable, able to teach, not addicted to wine or pugnacious, but gentle, peaceable, free from the love of money. He must be one who manages his own household well, keeping his children under control with all dignity (but if a man does not know how to manage his own household, how will he take care of the church of God?), and not a new convert, so that he will not become conceited and fall into the condemnation incurred by the devil. And he must have a good reputation with those outside the church, so that he may not fall into reproach and the snare of the devil." 1 Timothy 3:2-7

Review pages 67-83, 186-202.

6. "Above reproach" is the "general, overarching, all-embracing" qualification for a church elder. How would you answer the critic who asserts: "No one is above reproach!" "No one meets all the biblical qualifications for eldership, so you cannot insist upon elders meeting all these qualifications." (Also see pp. 228, 229.)

— means un-accused, one whose character is free from
— damaging moral or spiritual accusations
— one marred by no disgrace
— Not perfect, (but not controlled by sin)

7. Some elders earn their living in the business community. List the specific implications of being "above reproach" for this elder.

–Implications also apply to the community

8. A good deal of debate occurs over the qualification "the husband of one wife." Which interpretation of this qualification do you favor and why?

–once married / not divorced

Before you answer the next three questions, read the quotations below from John H. Armstrong's book, *Can Fallen Pastors Be Restored? The Church's Response to Sexual Misconduct*:

In 1988 *Leadership*, a journal read mostly by ministers, conducted a poll on the sexual practices of clergymen and printed the staggering results in an article titled, "How Common Is Pastoral Indiscretion?" Based on more than three hundred responses from its readership, their survey revealed the existence of a growing moral breakdown in pastors' lives. . . .

Twelve percent answered yes to the question: "Have you ever had sexual intercourse with someone other than your spouse since you have been in local-church ministry?". . . If these statistics are not frightening enough, 18 percent responded that they had engaged in "other forms of sexual contact with someone other than your spouse, i.e., passionate kissing, fondling/mutual masturbation," while in local-church ministry.

Similar research done by the Fuller Institute of Church Growth indicates that 37 percent of ministers "have been involved in inappropriate behavior with someone in the church." Harry W. Schaumburg, a therapist who works with problems of sexual misconduct and sexual addiction, adds . . . the following observation: "Evidence indicates that this shocking and disturbing statistic is true. I frequently receive calls for counseling from Christian leaders around the country who have 'fallen,' who are sexually addicted or have been involved in sexual misconduct. . . ."

The *Leadership* survey of pastors found that more than two-thirds of the pastors had become sexually involved with people from within the congregation, often serving in leadership roles within the local church. Asked for the major reason for this illicit relationship, respondents most often replied, "physical and emotional attraction." After reviewing these results, one prominent counseling professor at a major seminary said, "We're living in a Corinthian age, but we're preparing students for the Victorian age."

One religion editor, who devoted considerable study to this problem, recently wrote: "Experts who have studied clergy members' sexual misconduct believe at least one-third of all ministers have committed some type of sexual abuse on members of their congregations–and the rate could be higher."[2]

Sexual sin need not directly involve another person. An impure thought life of vicarious sex with real or imaginary partners can be equally damaging. Robertson McQuilkin maintains that "pornography destroys spiritually all who involve themselves in producing or using it, and its corrupting influence spills over into the entire life of the society that tolerates it."[3]

9. Why is it absolutely essential to the inner spiritual life and the external witness of the church that an elder's marital and sexual life be "above reproach"?

because the same attitudes of the elders will spill over to the church members.

10. According to Proverbs 6:27-35, what are the consequences of committing adultery? Be thorough in listing and understanding adultery's devastating consequences.

a. *scooping fire → get burned*

b. *touching adultress → will not go unpunished*

c. *a thief (even though starving) will still repay seven-fold*

d. *Disgrace*

e. *Shame never wiped away*

Church leaders are committing sexual sins and divorcing at epidemic rates. You can be certain that Satan will do everything in his power to ruin your marriage relationship and defile your sexual purity. Discuss with your mentor the problems and stresses you are experiencing in your marriage. Prior to this discussion, ask your wife for her viewpoint so that you can share her perspective.

Do not be afraid to talk about your marital frustrations–we all have them! What matters is how you handle your problems. People who have problems and solve them can help and comfort others. People who hide their marital sins and abuses, however, experience the deepest problems and bring disgrace to the Lord's name.

For elders, sexual sin usually does not begin as sexual temptation. Instead, it starts by our allowing intimacy to develop outside our marriage relationships. The man who puts his work ahead of his wife and, as a consequence, incurs her resentment of his ministry involvement, is the most vulnerable. The temptation to step across the line with another woman who appreciates him then becomes enormous.

Men need to receive respect and to believe that their work is significant. If their wives resent or belittle their ministries, men are tempted to look elsewhere for affirmation. If you are seeking appreciation or companionship from women other than your wife, you must step out of ministry and resolve your marital difficulties as your first priority. If you anticipate that the work of being an elder could lead to this temptation, you should not proceed until you have your wife's full and unreserved support.

To prevent the occurrence of inappropriate intimacy, elderships should have in place a strong accountability system. Randy Alcorn, in his booklet, *Sexual Temptation: How Christian Workers Can Win the Battle,* presents a plan for anticipating and preventing sexual temptations. It involves repeatedly reminding one's self and one's fellow brothers of the horrific consequences and costs of immorality.

Counting the Cost

"In 1850 Nathaniel Hawthorne published *The Scarlet Letter,* a powerful novel centered around the adulterous relationship of Hester Prynne and the highly respected minister, the Reverend Mr. Arthur Dimmesdale. The fallen pastor, remorseful but not ready to face the consequences, asks the question, 'What can a ruined soul, like mine, effect towards the redemption of other souls?–or a polluted soul, towards their purification?' He describes the misery of standing in his pulpit and seeing the admiration of his people, and having to 'then look inward, and discern the black reality of what they idolize.' Finally he says, 'I have laughed, in bitterness and agony of heart, at the contrast between what I seem and what I am! And Satan laughs at it!'

"[I asked] . . . a man who had been a leader in a Christian organization until he committed adultery, . . . 'What could have been done to prevent this?' He . . . said with haunting pain, 'If only I had really known, really thought through what it would cost me, my family and my Lord, I honestly believe I never would have done it.'

"Some years ago my copastor and friend Alan Hlavka and I each developed a list of all the specific consequences we could think of that would result from our immorality. The lists were devastating, and to us they spoke more powerfully than any sermon or article on the subject.

"Periodically . . . we read through this list. In a personal and tangible way it brings home God's inviolate law of choice and consequence. It cuts through the fog of rationalization and fills our hearts with the healthy, motivating fear of God. We find that when we begin to think unclearly, reviewing this list yanks us back to reality and the need both to fear God and the consequences of sin.

"What follows is an edited version of our combined lists. I've included the actual names of my wife and daughters to emphasize the personal nature of this exercise. I recommend that you use this as the basis for your own list, adding those other consequences that would be uniquely yours. The idea, of course, is to not focus on sin, but on the consequences of sin, thereby encouraging us to refocus on the Lord and take steps of wisdom and purity that can keep us from falling.

- ☐ Dragging Christ's reputation into the mud.
- ☐ Having to one day look Jesus in the face at the judgment seat and tell why I did it.
- ☐ Untold hurt to ~~Nanci~~ *Lynnéa*, my best friend and loyal wife. . . Loss of ~~Nanci~~'s *Lynnéa's* respect and trust.
- ☐ The possibility that I could lose my wife and my children forever.
- ☐ Hurt to and loss of credibility with my beloved daughters, ~~Karina and Angie~~ *Meyan & Carissa*. ('Why listen to a man who betrayed Mom and us?')
- ☐ Shame to my family. ('Why isn't Daddy a pastor anymore?' The cruel comments of others who would invariably find out.)
- ☐ Shame and hurt to my church and friends, and especially those I've led to Christ and discipled. (List names.)
- ☐ An irretrievable loss of years of witnessing to my father.
- ☐ Bringing great pleasure to Satan, God's enemy.
- ☐ Possibly contracting a sexually transmitted disease . . . [or causing] pregnancy, . . . (a lifelong reminder of sin to me and my family).
- ☐ Loss of self-respect, discrediting my own name, and invoking shame and lifelong embarrassment upon myself.

"This is less than half of the items from my list. If only we would rehearse in advance the ugly and overwhelming consequences of immorality, we would be far more prone to avoid it."

Randy C. Alcorn[4]

ASSIGNMENT:

Have a joint session with your mentor and your wife to talk about your shepherding ministry and its inevitable effect on your marriage. Be realistic about the fact that the pressures of being an elder will put your family at risk. Answer the following questions:

    a.　　Can you be an exemplary husband and also serve as an elder? *yes*

    b.　　Can your wife wholeheartedly support your ministry?　　*yes*

11.　Before you become an elder, you must clearly understand the biblical teaching on divorce and remarriage. You must be prepared to answer tough questions on these issues, and you must answer them biblically.

    a.　　Under what conditions is divorce permitted in your church?

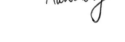 *Adultery*

    b.　　Under what conditions is remarriage permitted?

      7

    c.　　Are you in agreement with the church elders on these issues? If not, how will you work together and counsel others?　　*?*

ASSIGNMENT:

If you have not already completed an in-depth study of the biblical teaching on divorce and remarriage, begin studying this subject as soon as possible. Ask your elders to recommend a book or two that represent their view on divorce. This is a subject you must understand well in order to counsel others wisely.

12. The following five character qualities mentioned in 1 Timothy 3:2, 3 require careful attention. See pp. 193, 196-198.

    a. In your own words define the following qualities.

       Temperate:

       Prudent:

       Respectable:

       Not pugnacious:

       Peaceable:

    b. What do these qualities have in common?

13. What are the New Testament standards for a father that are required of a church elder? Check Titus 1:6 and pp. 229, 230.

    children who believe, are not open to the charge of wild & disobedient

"The Western world stands at a great crossroads in its history. It is my opinion that our very survival as a people will depend upon the presence or absence of masculine leadership in millions of homes. . . I believe, with everything within me, that husbands hold the keys to the preservation of the family."
James Dobson[5]

14. Eli was the priest over the house of the Lord at Shiloh. His two sons, Hophni and Phinehas, were also priests, but they were evil, lawless men. Eli made serious errors as a father that not only destroyed his sons, but destroyed his priestly ministry and the spiritual life of the nation. What were his errors in fathering? Read 1 Samuel 2:12-17, 22-36; 3:13.

a. *treating the sacrificed offerings of the people with contempt*

b. *slept with women who served*

c. *taking the choice parts of the sacrifice for themselves*

d.

15. After first addressing the question with your wife, discuss with your mentor the quality of your relationship with your children and where it needs improvement. Ask your children to honestly express their feelings about your fathering skills.

"Important as daily work may be, in the experience of the ordinary human being, the life of his family is far more important. His pride and his ambition may be involved in his professional advancement, but far more than pride and ambition are involved in his relationship to his *home*."[6]

"No matter how much a man may be concerned with his work in the world, he cannot normally *care* about it as much as he cares about his family. This is because we have, in the life of the family, a bigger stake than most of us can ever have in our employment. We can change business associates, if we need to, and we can leave a poor job for a better one, but we cannot change *sons*. If we lose the struggle in our occupational interests, we can try again, but if we lose with our children our loss is terribly and frighteningly *final*. A man who cares more for his work than he cares for his family is generally accounted abnormal or perverse and justifiably so. He is one who has not succeeded in getting his values straight; he fails to recognize what the true priorities are."

                                                                      Elton Trueblood[7]

16. Evaluate yourself in each of the following qualifications specified in 1 Timothy 3:2-7. Ask your wife or a close friend to make an independent evaluation of you as well.

a. A one-woman kind of man:

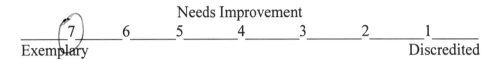

b. Temperate: a self-controlled, balanced man:

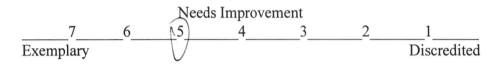

c. Prudent: a sensible man, of good judgment and discretion:

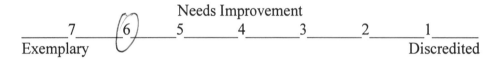

d. Respectable: an orderly, disciplined, honorable man:

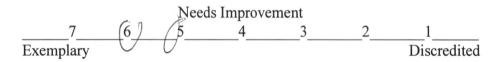

e. Hospitable:

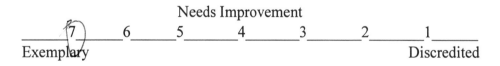

f. Able to teach: meaning a man who is able to instruct others from the Bible:

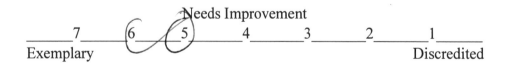

g. Not addicted to wine: a man whose habits and lifestyle do not damage his testimony:

h.   Not pugnacious: a man whose temper and emotions are in check:

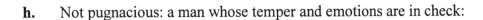

                                              Needs Improvement

_____7_____ 6_____ 5_____ 4_____ 3_____ 2_____ 1_____
Exemplary   Discredited

i.   Gentle: a forbearing, gracious, conciliatory man:

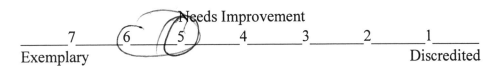

                                              Needs Improvement

_____7_____ 6_____ 5_____ 4_____ 3_____ 2_____ 1_____
Exemplary   Discredited

j.   Peaceable: an uncontentious man, one who is not quarrelsome:

                                              Needs Improvement

_____7_____ 6_____ 5_____ 4_____ 3_____ 2_____ 1_____
Exemplary   Discredited

k.   Free from the love of money: meaning a man who is not materialistic:

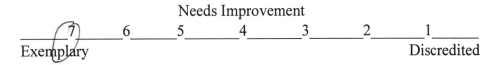

                                            Needs Improvement

_____7_____ 6_____ 5_____ 4_____ 3_____ 2_____ 1_____
Exemplary   Discredited

l.   A man who manages his household well: a responsible Christian father, husband, and household manager:

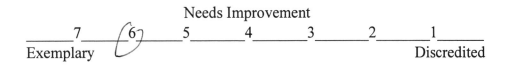

                                            Needs Improvement

_____7_____ 6_____ 5_____ 4_____ 3_____ 2_____ 1_____
Exemplary   Discredited

m.   Not a new convert: a man who is spiritually mature, tested:

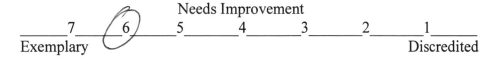

                                          Needs Improvement

_____7_____ 6_____ 5_____ 4_____ 3_____ 2_____ 1_____
Exemplary   Discredited

n.   A man with a good reputation outside the Christian community:

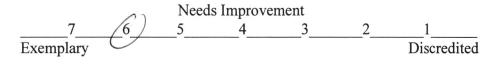

                                          Needs Improvement

_____7_____ 6_____ 5_____ 4_____ 3_____ 2_____ 1_____
Exemplary   Discredited

Scripture Memory Assignment:

"It is a trustworthy statement: if any man aspires to the office of overseer, it is a fine work he desires to do. An overseer, then, must be above reproach, the husband of one wife, temperate, prudent, respectable, hospitable, able to teach, not addicted to wine or pugnacious, but gentle, peaceable, free from the love of money. He must be one who manages his own household well, keeping his children under control with all dignity (but if a man does not know how to manage his own household, how will he take care of the church of God?), and not a new convert, so that he will not become conceited and fall into the condemnation incurred by the devil. And he must have a good reputation with those outside the church, so that he may not fall into reproach and the snare of the devil."   1 Timothy 3:1-7

---

[1] An excellent example is John MacArthur's series on 1 Timothy, which may be ordered from Grace to You, P. O. Box 4000, Panorama City, California, 91412. Call 1-800-554-7223.

[2] John H. Armstrong, *Can Fallen Pastors Be Restored? The Church's Response to Sexual Misconduct* (Chicago: Moody, 1995), pp. 19, 20.

[3] Robertson McQuilkin, *An Introduction to Biblical Ethics* (Wheaton: Tyndale, 1989), p. 237. We encourage all elders to purchase and read McQuilkin's book. It interacts with all the major contemporary ethical issues. Wise men need to read books like this one to help them think critically and biblically and to be able to answer questions about ethical issues.

[4] Randy C. Alcorn, *Sexual Temptation: How Christian Workers Can Win the Battle* (Gresham: Eternal Perspective Ministries, 1995), pp. 28-30.

[5] James C. Dobson, *Straight Talk to Men and Their Wives* (Waco: Word, 1980), p. 21.

[6] Elton Trueblood, *Your Other Vocation* (New York: Harper and Row, 1952), p. 80.

[7] Ibid., p. 82.

LESSON 8

HONORING AND DISCIPLINING ELDERS

LESSON OVERVIEW

Lesson 8 surveys 1 Timothy 5:17-25, one of the most significant New Testament passages on the doctrine of Christian eldership. It focuses on elders who deserve double honor because of their capable leadership and diligent labor in the Word and explains the necessity of evaluating each elder's gifts.

The passage also addresses the difficult issue of disciplining elders who have been proved guilty of sin. The lesson emphasizes the need for leaders to be courageous in exposing sin, to judge justly, and to follow the New Testament precautions in appointing elders.

ELDERS DESERVING DOUBLE HONOR

"The elders who rule well are to be considered worthy of double honor, especially those who work hard at preaching and teaching. For the Scripture says, 'You shall not muzzle the ox while he is threshing,' and 'The laborer is worthy of his wages.'"
1 Timothy 5:17, 18

Read pages 206-215.

---

1. What unique, significant contributions does 1 Timothy 5:17, 18 make to our understanding of the New Testament doctrine of eldership?

preaching the word takes an immense amount of time & energy (physical, mental, emotional, spiritual) for that reason, we are to doubly honor those who work hard at preaching.

2. Since all elders are involved in leading the local church, what distinguishes those elders who "rule well"?

those who are putting effort into leading people in their spiritual growth

3. How does *Biblical Eldership* explain the fact that all elders must be able to teach, but some elders labor at teaching and thus are entitled to financial support?

Not all preach, this verse seems to indicate or emphasize preaching & the significant time/energy factor needed.

4. Note the close connection between leading and teaching that is made in 1 Timothy 5:17. In what sense does one who teaches the Word also lead?

* people will always follow teachers & those who visibly lead (good or bad). - people look to the teacher

5. Ephesians 4:11 mentions the spiritual gift of "pastor" ("shepherd"). Describe this gift and explain why it is important to the eldership.

v.12 to prepare God's people for works of service so that the body of Christ may be built up until all reach faith & maturity

Below is a list of spiritual gifts that are particularly helpful in making the eldership team effective in shepherding.

- **"Administrations"** (1 Cor. 12:28): A much better translation of the Greek (*kybernēsis*) would be "acts of guidance," that is, able to provide wise counsel and direction for the congregation. Look up Proverbs 11:14 and 24:6, where this same term is translated as "guidance."

- **Leading** (Rom. 12:8): This is the Greek word *prohistēmi,* which we have noted several times. Refer to the exposition of 1 Thessalonians 5:12, 13 for an explanation of this term (pp. 167, 168, and lesson 5).

- **Exhorting** (Rom. 12:8): Exhorting could also mean "consoling" or "encouraging." Quoting Martin Luther, Leon Morris writes, "'The teacher transmits knowledge; the exhorter stimulates.'"[1]

- **Shepherding** (Eph. 4:11): In this verse the Greek noun for "pastors" is *poimenas*, which means "shepherds." The noun *poimenas* is used only this once in Scripture to describe Christian leaders. The English word *pastor,* which is now erroneously used as a title, comes from the Latin translation of *poimenas. Pastor* is a spiritual gift; it is not an office separate from or superior to the office of elder. The elders are given the mandate to jointly pastor God's flock, and some elders have the spiritual gift of shepherding (pp. 149, 210, 211, *Biblical Eldership*). We have no scriptural precedent for calling some men in the local church "pastors" in distinction from the elders.

- **Teaching** (Eph. 4:11)

- **Evangelizing** (Eph. 4:11)

- **Showing mercy** (Rom. 12:8)

6. How do we know that the word *honor* (Greek, *timē*) in 1 Timothy 5:17 includes the sense of financial maintenance?

    a. *You shall not muzzle the ox while he is threshing*

    b. *The laborer is worthy of his wages*

7. In light of past problems at Ephesus, why is Paul particularly concerned that the elders who labor in the Word be financially supported by the church?

ASSIGNMENTS:

An important question that an elder must continually ask regarding full- or part-time service is: how does he view himself in relation to the other elders, and how do the other elders view him? If your church has salaried elders and tentmaking elders, ask the different parties the above questions. Request scriptural support for their answers.

Also ask about the tensions and problems that naturally emerge between salaried elders who serve full or part time and tentmaking elders. Discuss this issue with your mentor.

Complete the Gifts Analysis Questionnaire, *"Discover Your Gifts,"* at the end of this lesson.

a.   What special contribution do you think your gift or gifts can make to the eldership team?

b.   What are you presently doing to distinguish, develop, and employ your spiritual gift(s)?

PROTECTING AND DISCIPLINING ELDERS

"Do not receive an accusation against an elder except on the basis of two or three witnesses. Those who continue in sin, rebuke in the presence of all, so that the rest also may be fearful of sinning. I solemnly charge you in the presence of God and of Christ Jesus and of His chosen angels, to maintain these principles without bias, doing nothing in a spirit of partiality. Do not lay hands upon anyone too hastily and thereby share responsibility for the sins of others; keep yourself free from sin. No longer drink water exclusively, but use a little wine for the sake of your stomach and your frequent ailments. The sins of some men are quite evident, going before them to judgment; for others, their sins follow after. Likewise also, deeds that are good are quite evident, and those which are otherwise cannot be concealed."

1 Timothy 5:19-25

Read pages 215-224.

 8.   Why does Paul require that elders receive specific protection from unsubstantiated accusations?

 9.   It is important that elders understand the legal principle, "on the evidence of two or three witnesses:"

a.   What is the origin of this principle?

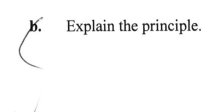 b. Explain the principle.

c. Why is it essential that elders follow this legal principle?

 10. What is the main point of Paul's instruction concerning an elder who has sinned?

11. Note Paul's charge to Timothy:

   a. What does Paul say to show his serious intentions about openness and fairness when judging an accusation of sin, or the actual sin, of a church elder?

   b. What is implied by the intensity of Paul's language?

12. What will be the consequence for us if we disobey Paul's charge to judge other elders openly and fairly?

13. What are the consequences for the elder council if they are too hasty in restoring an elder or in appointing an unqualified or untested elder?

"The faculty of keeping an open mind until all the facts and circumstances bearing upon a question have been ascertained is by no means common, and yet for the right guidance and management of complex affairs, it is obviously essential. I have had occasion repeatedly to observe that individuals gifted in some respects are sadly lacking in the quality mentioned; and yet unless the one in a central position is careful to hear and weigh all that has to be said touching the different aspect of a given affair, he will not be in a position either to reach a sound conclusion or to carry with him the consent and confidence of those affected by that conclusion."

D. E. Hoste[2]

14. As a spiritual leader, you will be called upon to make judgments about people and their circumstances. In a sinful, unjust world, this is a difficult job. When dealing with relatives and close friends, even the most reputable Christians can be guilty of bias or of believing only one side of a story. Read the following verses and list the biblical principles that will help you judge people fairly and objectively.

Prov. 18:13 He who gives an answer before he hears, it is folly and shame to him.

Prov. 18:17 The first to plead his case seems just [right], until another comes and examines him.

Lev. 19:15 "You shall do no injustice in judgment; you shall not be partial to the poor nor defer to the great, but you are to judge your neighbor fairly."

2 Chron. 19:6, 7 He [King Jehoshaphat] said to the judges, "Consider what you are doing, for you do not judge for man but for the Lord who is with you when you render judgment. Now then let the fear of the Lord be upon you; be very careful what you do, for the Lord our God will have no part in unrighteousness or partiality or the taking of a bribe."

Job 29:16 "I was a father to the needy, and I investigated the case which I did not know."

Isa. 61:8a For I, the Lord, love justice, I hate robbery in the burnt offering; and I will faithfully give them their recompense.

John 7:51 "Our Law does not judge a man unless it first hears from him and knows what he is doing, does it?"

a.

b.

c.

Let us share some sound advice: keep records whenever you are involved in delicate matters, disputes, or judging cases of church discipline. We tend to avoid recording unpleasant facts, but that can prove unwise. Many elders have been saved from serious misunderstandings and false accusations by having accurate records of phone conversations, meetings, and events. On several occasions, we have been able to produce facts and records for people who questioned how our churches handled the discipline of members who later accused us of mishandling their situation (a charge unrepentant sinners make against those who confront and deal with their sin).

In sensitive, painful situations that require the judgment and wise counsel of the elders, it is easy to forget what was said and what was decided. All decisions and judgments made by the elders should be accurately recorded so that valuable time is not wasted in recalling past decisions.

15. What qualifications enable an elder to judge sinning members fairly and objectively? Explain your answers.

1 Timothy 3:2-7

1. Above reproach
2. The husband of one wife
3. Temperate [self-controlled, balanced]
4. Prudent [sensible, good judgment]
5. Respectable [well-behaved, virtuous]
6. Hospitable
7. Able to teach
8. Not addicted to wine
9. Not pugnacious [not belligerent]
10. Gentle [forbearing]
11. Peaceable [uncontentious]
12. Free from the love of money
13. Manages his household well
14. Not a new convert
15. A good reputation with those outside the church

Titus 1:6-9

1. Above reproach
2. The husband of one wife
3. Having children who believe
4. Not self-willed
5. Not quick-tempered
6. Not addicted to wine
7. Not pugnacious
8. Not fond of sordid gain
9. Hospitable
10. Lover of what is good [kind, virtuous]
11. Sensible [see prudent]
12. Just [righteous conduct, law-abiding]
13. Devout [holy, pleasing to God, loyal to His Word]
14. Self-controlled
15. Holds fast the faithful [trustworthy NIV] Word, both to exhort and to refute

1 Peter 5:1-3

1. Not shepherding under compulsion, but voluntarily
2. Not shepherding for sordid gain, but with eagerness
3. Not lording it over the flock, but proving to be an example

a.

b.

c.

16. Confronting and rebuking a fellow elder (or anyone else) who is sinning requires a fearless spirit. If you, like most of us, lack the courage to exercise church discipline, read the following Scripture texts in their context and explain what you learn about this important leadership virtue. Discover the importance of courage on pp. 20-22.

Josh. 1:6-9

2 Sam. 10:12

1 Chron. 28:20

Ezra 10:4

Ezek. 2:6, 7

Amos 7:10-17

John 2:13-22

Acts 15:1, 2

Gal. 2:11-14

17. One unfit elder can cause untold trouble for a church and bring havoc on the eldership. In order to prevent unqualified and unworthy men from becoming elders, the Spirit of God gives invaluable counsel to the church family on selecting and examining a prospective elder.

a. Since the warning, "Do not lay hands upon anyone too hastily," comes after instruction on rebuking an elder who has been found guilty of sin, what does 1 Tim. 5:22 imply about the restoration of such an elder?

b. Write an expanded paraphrase and explanation of 1 Tim. 3:10. (See pp. 76, 77, 202-204.)

c. Explain how each of the following statements from 1 Tim. 5:24, 25 encourages and guides the local church and its elders in examining potential elders.

"The sins of some men are quite evident, going before them to judgment," v. 24*a*.

"For others, their sins follow after," v. 24*b*.

"Likewise also, deeds that are good are quite evident," v. 25*a*.

"And those which are otherwise [not evident] cannot be concealed," v. 25*b*.

ASSIGNMENT:

Since you must someday be examined by the church and its elders as to your lifestyle, abilities, and doctrine (1 Tim. 3:10), ask the elders now for a list of questions and issues they will cover at that time.

18. Here are key questions you should answer personally in order to prepare yourself for examination:

 a. How long have you been in your present local church?

 b. Do you agree with the church's doctrinal positions?

 c. How well do the congregation and elders know you?

 d. How do you know they have confidence in you?

 e. Is there anything in your past or present moral lifestyle that, if it became known, would bring reproach on the church or the eldership?

 f. In what ministries have you exercised your giftedness?

 g. What have you done to train for eldership?

SCRIPTURE MEMORY ASSIGNMENT:

"Do not receive an accusation against an elder except on the basis of two or three witnesses. Those who continue in sin, rebuke in the presence of all, so that the rest also may be fearful of sinning. I solemnly charge you in the presence of God and of Christ Jesus and of His chosen angels, to maintain these principles without bias, doing nothing in a spirit of partiality." 1 Timothy 5:19-21

---

[1] Leon Morris, *The Epistle to the Romans* (Grand Rapids: Eerdmans, 1988), pp. 441, 442.
[2] D. E. Hoste, *If I Am to Lead* (London: Overseas Missionary Fellowship, 1968), p. 7.

DISCOVER YOUR GIFTS - GIFTS ANALYSIS QUESTIONNAIRE

Each statement in the following questionnaire has five response spaces following it: very little, little, some, much, very much. These represent percentages on a scale of 1-100%, as follows:

Very little   = 0 - 20%
Little   = 20 - 40%
Some   = 40 - 60%
Much   = 60 - 80%
Very much = 80 - 100%

Read each statement. Decide to what extent the statement is true of you. Check the appropriate column. Your first impressions are usually correct. If most of your checks are placed toward the right or toward the left, don't worry about that. Each person has his own style with questionnaires. The questionnaire will help you discover your gifts. The results of this questionnaire will be only tentative, however.

THE FOLLOWING IS TRUE OF ME

	1 Very Little	2 Little	3 Some	4 Much	5 Very Much
1. I am able to organize ideas, tasks, people, and time, for Christian service.			X		
2. I have used a particular creative ability (writing, painting, drama, etc.) to benefit the body of Christ.	X				
3. I am able to distinguish between spiritual truth and error.				X	X
4. I have been used to encourage people to live Christlike lives.				X	
5. I like to talk about Jesus to those who don't know him.			X		
6. I have had the experience of knowing God's will with certainty in a specific situation even when concrete evidence was missing.			X		
7. I assume responsibility for meeting financial needs in church and community.				X	
8. I enjoy providing a haven for guests and do not feel put upon by unexpected visitors.					X
9. I take prayer requests of others seriously and continue to pray for them.				X	
10. I motivate groups toward specific biblical objectives.				X	
11. I have a knack for turning compassion into cheerful deeds of kindness.		X			
12. I have pleaded the cause of God to the people of the church and/or world.		X			
13. I enjoy doing tasks that help others minister effectively.			X		

LESSON 8

THE FOLLOWING IS TRUE OF ME

	1 Very Little	2 Little	3 Some	4 Much	5 Very Much
14. I have been responsible for the spiritual lives of Christians with good results.	☐	☐	☒	☐	☐
15. Content "comes alive" for students (children or adults) when I teach.	☐	☐	☒	☐	☐
16. I like to plan things in which people are involved.	☐	☐	☐	☒	☐
17. I would enjoy expressing myself creatively for God through artistic expression (music, drama, poetry, etc.).	☒	☐	☐	☐	☐
18. I see a serious danger when false teachings and false practices creep into the church.	☐	☐	☐	☐	☒
19. I am sensitive to suffering, troubled, and discouraged people, and want to help them see God's answers to life's problems.	☐	☒	☐	☐	☐
20. I would like to be able to share the gospel freely and effectively with unbelieving persons.	☐	☐	☒	☐	☐
21. I find myself accepting God's promises at face value and applying them to given situations without doubt.	☐	☐	☐	☒	☐
22. I feel moved to give when confronted with financial needs in God's kingdom.	☐	☐	☐	☐	☒
23. I am sensitive to the acts of kindness which make such a difference for guests or strangers.	☐	☐	☒	☐	☐
24. I am sensitive to the prayer needs of others and concerned to give the needed prayer support.	☐	☐	☐	☒	☐
25. I have a desire to help, lead, guide, and direct people in an important church ministry.	☐	☐	☐	☒	☐
26. I would like to minister to those who have physical or mental problems.	☐	☒	☐	☐	☐
27. I have spiritual insights from the Scriptures relating to people and issues which make me want to speak out.	☐	☐	☐	☒	☐
28. I sense when others need a helping hand and am ready to give it.	☐	☐	☒	☐	☐
29. I desire to see the spiritual needs of believers met and I am willing to be personally involved in nurturing and discipling ministries.	☐	☐	☐	☒	☐
30. I like to help people understand things.	☐	☐	☐	☒	☐
31. I am able to make effective plans to accomplish goals.	☐	☐	☒	☐	☐
32. I have significant artistic ability (music, drama, writing, painting, sculpting, etc.) which I have put to good use in God's kingdom.	☒	☐	☐	☐	☐

THE FOLLOWING IS TRUE OF ME

	1 Very Little	2 Little	3 Some	4 Much	5 Very Much
33. I have detected phony or manipulative persons and teachings when others have not.	☐	☐	☒	☒	☐
34. People in the Christian community have been stirred up to love and good works by my counsel and encouragement.	☐	☐	☒	☐	☐
35. I have been instrumental in leading others to believe in Christ as their Savior.	☐	☐	☒	☐	☐
36. In specific cases God has given me assurance that he would do what seemed unlikely.	☐	☐	☒	☐	☐
37. I give cheerfully and liberally in support of the Lord's work.	☐	☐	☐	☒	☐
38. I have a knack for making strangers feel at ease in my home and at church.	☐	☐	☐	☒	☐
39. I pray for others, recognizing that their effectiveness depends upon it.	☐	☐	☒	☐	☐
40. I enjoy leading and directing others toward goals and caring for them for the sake of Christ.	☐	☐	☐	☒	☐
41. I enjoy working with people who suffer physical, mental or emotional problems.	☒	☐	☐	☐	☐
42. I have proclaimed timely and urgent messages from God's Word.	☐	☒	☐	☐	☐
43. I like to work at little things that help build the body of Christ.	☐	☐	☒	☐	☐
44. I assume responsibility when I see a Christian being led astray.	☐	☐	☐	☒	☐
45. I am able to clarify things for learners (children or adults).	☐	☐	☒	☐	☐
46. I would enjoy giving oversight to an important church ministry.	☐	☐	☐	☒	☐
47. I have the potential to be very creative in an area that could be used in building up the church.	☒	☐	☐	☐	☐
48. I tend to look beneath the surface and perceive people's motives.	☐	☐	☐	☒	☐
49. I believe that people will grow to spiritual maturity through counsel and instruction from the Word.	☐	☐	☐	☐	☒
50. I have a burden for friends and acquaintances who do not believe in Christ.	☐	☐	☐	☒	☐
51. I have a sense for moments when the "prayer of faith" is needed.	☐	☐	☒	☐	☐

LESSON 8

	1 Very Little	2 Little	3 Some	4 Much	5 Very Much

THE FOLLOWING IS TRUE OF ME

#	Statement	1	2	3	4	5
52.	I am willing to maintain a lower standard of living in order to benefit God's work with my financial support.	☐	☐	☒	☐	☐
53.	I tend to be more aware of the needs of guests than of my own.	☐	☐	☐	☒	☐
54.	I have an inner conviction that God works in response to prayer, and I want to be used to help others through prayer.	☐	☐	☐	☒	☐
55.	If I had the opportunity, I would enjoy leading, directing, and motivating others in some aspect of the Lord's work.	☐	☐	☐	☒	☐
56.	The sight of misery makes me want to find a way to express God's love to hurting persons.	☐	☐	☐	☒	☐
57.	Given the opportunity, I would like to be an expository preacher of God's Word.	☐	☐	☒	☐	☐
58.	It is my nature to like to do work that helps others do theirs.	☐	☐	☒	☐	☐
59.	I sense in myself a shepherd's instinct when I know of Christians who need spiritual counsel.	☐	☐	☐	☒	☐
60.	I quickly sense when people (children or adults) are unclear in their thinking.	☐	☐	☒	☒	☐
61.	I have a sense for delegating important tasks to the right people at the right time.	☐	☐	☒	☐	☐
62.	I am aware that people have been blessed through my creative or artistic ability.	☒	☐	☐	☐	☐
63.	I have developed an ability to discriminate between good and evil in today's world.	☐	☐	☐	☒	☐
64.	I am glad when people who need comfort, consolation, encouragement, and counsel seek my help.	☐	☐	☒	☐	☐
65.	I am able to share the gospel in a way that makes it clear and meaningful to non-believers.	☐	☒	☒	☐	☐
66.	I am able to go on believing God will act in a situation in spite of evidence to the contrary.	☐	☐	☐	☒	☐
67.	I help people and the Lord's work through generous and timely contributions.	☐	☐	☐	☒	☐
68.	My home is available to those in need of hospitality.	☐	☐	☐	☒	☐
69.	I am conscious of ministering to others as I pray for them.	☐	☐	☐	☒	☐
70.	I have accepted leadership responsibilities and have succeeded in helping a group work toward a goal.	☐	☐	☐	☒	☐

THE FOLLOWING IS TRUE OF ME	1 Very Little	2 Little	3 Some	4 Much	5 Very Much
71. Sick, helpless, and shut-in persons are helped when I minister to them.	☐	☒	☐	☐	☐
72. God uses me to build up, encourage, and comfort other Christians by speaking to them of spiritual things.	☐	☐	☒	☐	☐
73. I find practical ways of helping others and gain satisfaction from doing this.	☐	☒	☐	☐	☐
74. The Lord has used me to watch over, guide, and nurture other believers toward spiritual maturity.	☐	☐	☐	☒	☐
75. I hold the interest of those I teach.	☐	☐	☒	☐	☐
76. I have a sense for how and when projects or ministries need to be better organized.	☐	☐	☐	☒	☐
77. I sense a latent creative ability (in drawing, writing, music, etc.) which I would like to use for the kingdom of God.	☒	☐	☐	☐	☐
78. I am usually aware of people who pretend to be what they are not.	☐	☐	☐	☒	☐
79. I would be willing to spend some time each week in a counseling ministry.	☐	☒	☐	☐	☐
80. I am able to sense when a person doesn't know Jesus Christ, and I hurt for him or her.	☐	☐	☒	☐	☐
81. I inwardly sense what Jesus meant when he said mountains could be moved by faith.	☐	☐	☒	☐	☐
82. I have a conviction that all I have belongs to God, and I want to be a good steward.	☐	☐	☐	☒	☐
83. I have a genuine appreciation for each guest to whom I minister.	☐	☐	☐	☒	☐
84. I would be pleased if asked to be a prayer partner to someone involved in a ministry.	☐	☐	☐	☒	☐
85. I am usually quick to sense when a group I am a part of is "spinning its wheels," and I want to do something about it.	☐	☐	☐	☒	☐
86. I sense when people are hurting in some way.	☐	☐	☐	☒	☐
87. I think more Christians should speak out on the moral issues of the day, such as abortion, easy sex, racism, and so on.	☐	☐	☐	☒	☐
88. I wish I had more opportunity to assist others in their ministries.	☐	☐	☒	☐	☐
89. I would love to be in a position to equip saints for the work of ministry.	☐	☐	☐	☒	☐
90. I get excited about discovering new ideas I can share with others.	☐	☐	☐	☒	☐

When you have finished the Key Chart on page 19, continue by reading the following questions and answers.

1. **Do I actually have the spiritual gifts I have identified?**

   Some people are surprised by the gifts which their questionnaire reveals; others are not. Whichever category you fall into, two things must be said. First, congratulations! To be aware of gifts which the Holy Spirit gives is an exciting experience, and very significant.

   Second, be cautious. You may not actually have the spiritual gifts you identify by taking this questionnaire. Or you may have other gifts not identified here. Two more things should happen before you will be sure what your gifts really are:

   a. Others should observe your gifts and tell you what you do well.

   b. You should actually use your gifts in ministries and experience a degree of success.

2. **What is the difference between a working gift and a waiting gift?**

   A working gift is a gift you are already using in some way. You may not have recognized it as a spiritual gift, but you were using it nonetheless. You were able to identify working gifts by answering questions aimed at your activities in the kingdom.

   A waiting gift, on the other hand, is a gift which remains to a large extent undeveloped. There may be hints of it in your activities, but for the most part you haven't used it. However, you do have potential in this area. You cannot identify such a gift simply by looking at activities. Instead you must look at interests, inclinations, sensitivities, attitudes, and concerns. These often reveal a gift *waiting* to be developed.

3. **What am I to do in those areas where I don't have gifts?**

   Don't think less of yourself because of those gifts which appear in box C, which for you are not gifts but roles. Remember that others have been given gifts in these areas for your sake. Thank God for these gifts and those who have them. In addition, you should encourage and pray for those who have these gifts: they are important to God and his cause. They need the support which you, with *your* gifts, can give them. Finally, you have a responsibility to be diligent in each of these areas as a member of the church. For example, if evangelism is last on your list, you should recognize that while God may not expect you to be involved in door-to-door visitation, you still have a responsibility to witness.

Discover Your Gifts - Gifts Analysis Questionnaire
Church Development Resources ™
A Ministry of CRC Publications
2850 Kalamazoo Ave. SE
Grand Rapids, MI 49560
Copyright © 1989

LESSON 8

HOW TO USE THE KEY CHART

Complete the Key Chart on your own. Begin by reading the instructions carefully.

1. Place the numerical value (1-5) for each statement of the questionnaire (1-90) next to the corresponding number in the Key Chart.

2. In Chart A, add each row of three numbers, and write the total in the adjoining box in the "totals A" column. Do the same in "totals B" column for Chart B, adding to the left.

3. Circle the highest scores in the "totals A" column. Circle three or four, but not more than five. Write the names of those gifts in box A, "Working Gifts," with the highest-scored gift first, the next highest second. (In case of ties, it doesn't matter which one is listed first.)

4. Now in the "totals B" column circle the high scores which were not circled in step 3. Write these gifts in box B, "Waiting Gifts," beginning with the highest.

5. Place in box C any gifts not listed in boxes A and B. These are not likely to be your spiritual gifts, but you have, of course, a responsibility (role) in each of them.

6. Note the gifts in which your "totals B" score is significantly (two or more) higher than your "totals A" score. This may indicate a gift you should develop and use.

CHART A			Totals A	Totals B	CHART B		
1 — 3	31 — 3	61 — 3	Administration 9	12	16 — 4	46 — 4	76 — 4
2 — 1	32 — 1	62 — 1	Creative Ability 3	3	17 — 1	47 — 1	77 — 1
3 — 5	33 — 4	63 — 4	Discernment 13	13	18 — 5	48 — 4	78 — 4
4 — 4	34 — 3	64 — 3	Encouragement 10	9	19 — 2	49 — 5	79 — 2
5 — 3	35 — 3	65 — 2	Evangelism 8	10	20 — 3	50 — 4	80 — 3
6 — 3	36 — 3	66 — 4	Faith 10	10	21 — 4	51 — 3	81 — 3
7 — 4	37 — 4	67 — 4	Giving 12	12	22 — 5	52 — 3	82 — 4
8 — 5	38 — 4	68 — 4	Hospitality 13	11	23 — 3	53 — 4	83 — 4
9 — 4	39 — 3	69 — 4	Intercession 11	12	24 — 4	54 — 4	84 — 4
10 — 4	40 — 4	70 — 4	Leadership 12	12	25 — 4	55 — 4	85 — 4
11 — 2	41 — 1	71 — 2	Mercy 5	10	26 — 2	56 — 4	86 — 4
12 — 2	42 — 2	72 — 3	Prophecy 7	11	27 — 4	57 — 3	87 — 4
13 — 3	43 — 3	73 — 2	Service 8	9	28 — 3	58 — 3	88 — 3
14 — 3	44 — 4	74 — 4	Shepherding 11	12	29 — 4	59 — 4	89 — 4
15 — 3	45 — 3	75 — 3	Teaching 9	12	30 — 4	60 — 4	90 — 4

Box A Working Gifts
(Highest scored gifts)

1st Discernment
2nd Hospitality
3rd Giving
4th Leadership
5th Shepherding / Intercession

Box B Waiting Gifts
(Highest scored gifts, not in Box A)

1st Discernment
2nd Giving 12
3rd Administration 12
4th Leadership 12
5th Intercession 12

Box C Not a gift but a role (responsibility)

_____ _____ _____ _____
_____ _____ _____ _____

LESSON 9

APPOINT ONLY QUALIFIED MEN

LESSON OVERVIEW

Lesson 9 reviews Paul's instructions to Titus and the underdeveloped churches on the Island of Crete that were facing attack from false teachers. Paul sets forth the qualifications for elders: church elders must control personal anger, be hospitable, be faithful to Christian doctrine, and be able to exhort in sound doctrine and refute false teachers. The lesson also examines the terms "ordination" and "appointment," and the unbiblical division between clergy and laity.

PAUL'S INSTRUCTIONS TO TITUS

"For this reason I left you in Crete, that you would set in order what remains and appoint elders in every city as I directed you." Titus 1:5

Review pages 104-106. Read pages 202-205, 225-228.

1. One cannot grasp the significance of Paul's teaching on elders without first understanding the reasons why he wrote to Timothy and Titus.

    a. What evidence is there that these letters were not strictly personal correspondence, but that they conveyed teachings that applied to all the churches?

    b.   What is the purpose of these letters?

2.   Describe Titus's and Timothy's position and mission (pp. 104, 105, 204, 205).

3.   Paul's choice of terminology in Titus 1:5-9 reveals important information about elder appointment. Consider the meaning and significance of Paul's terms.

    a.   What is the meaning of the verb *kathistēmi,* translated "appoint"?

    b.   What is the meaning of the verb *diatassō,* translated "directed"?

    c.   What is the essence of Paul's instruction to Titus in Titus 1:5-9?

ELDER QUALIFICATIONS

"Namely, if any man is above reproach, the husband of one wife, having children who believe, not accused of dissipation or rebellion. For the overseer must be above reproach as God's steward, not self-willed, not quick-tempered, not addicted to wine, not pugnacious, not fond of sordid gain, but hospitable, loving what is good, sensible, just, devout, self-controlled, holding fast the faithful word which is in accordance with the teaching, so that he will be able both to exhort in sound doctrine and to refute those who contradict. For there are many rebellious men, empty talkers and deceivers, especially those of the circumcision, who must be silenced because they are upsetting whole families, teaching things they should not teach for the sake of sordid gain."
                                              Titus 1:6-11

Review pages 228-238.

 4. There is disagreement over the meaning of the Greek term *pistos*, "having children who believe," in Titus 1:6. Describe the opposing viewpoints and indicate the one you prefer and why.

    a.

    b.

    c.

        1

        2

        3

 5. Paul uses the Greek noun *oikonomos* ("steward") to identify the elder's function in the church.

     a. What does *oikonomos* mean?

    b. What does an *oikonomos* do (p. 70)?

    c. What does the term *oikonomos* tell you about an elder's identity and work?

    d. What does the fact that elders are God's *oikonomoi* teach you about elders?

e. Explain how the term *oikonomos* bolsters Paul's major point that the elder has to be qualified for office.

> "God has revealed to us that one of His own attributes is that He is slow to anger. A calm and patient spirit in the presence of wrong and injustice should be cultivated by every Christian man; but it is specially needful in the case of those entrusted with the high honour of preaching the Gospel or exercising oversight amongst the Lord's people. 'The beginning of strife is like the letting out of water.' It is of vital importance, therefore, if at any time we find ourselves tempted to enter into contention, that we should seek for grace to be kept from doing so, and give ourselves to quiet waiting upon the Lord for His power and guidance. In no other way can we be fitted to deal with the faults and disputes of others without ourselves becoming infected with the spirit of strife and partisanship."
>
> D. E. Hoste[1]

6. Uncontrolled anger ruins relationships, crushes the spirit, and divides churches and eldership teams. Unsanctified anger is a grave evil, especially in a leader (1 Sam. 20:30-34). Anger must always be controlled and channeled properly.

   a. According to the following Scripture passages, what are the character traits of a man who controls his anger?

   Prov. 14:17a A quick-tempered man acts foolishly.

   Prov. 14:29 He who is slow to anger has great understanding, but he who is quick-tempered exalts folly.

   Prov. 15:18 A hot-tempered man stirs up strife, but the slow to anger pacifies a contention.

   Prov. 19:11 A man's discretion makes him slow to anger, and it is his glory to overlook a transgression.

   Prov. 29:11 A fool always loses his temper, but a wise man holds it back.

   Eph. 4:26, 27 Be angry, and yet do not sin; do not let the sun go down on your anger, and do not give the devil an opportunity.

James 1:19, 20 **This you know, my beloved brethren. But everyone must be quick to hear, slow to speak and slow to anger; for the anger of man does not achieve the righteousness of God.**

b. Using what you have gleaned from *Biblical Eldership* (pp. 232, 233) and the verses above, explain why a quick-tempered, angry man does not qualify to be an elder.

7. To deliver yourself from much unnecessary conflict and emotional stress, memorize and practice Proverbs 15:1:

A gentle answer turns away wrath,
But a harsh word stirs up anger.

a. What does "a gentle answer turns away wrath" mean? Give an example from your own experience with people that illustrates this principle.

Meaning:

Example:

b. What does "a harsh word stirs up anger" mean? Give an example from your own experience with people that illustrates this principle.

Meaning:

Example:

"The biblical shepherd is a shepherd of people–God's precious, blood-bought people. And like Christ, the Chief Shepherd, the church shepherd must give himself lovingly and sacrificially for the care of God's people (1 Thess. 2:8). This cannot be done from a distance, with a smile and a handshake on Sunday morning or through a superficial visit. Giving oneself to the care of God's people means sharing one's life and home with others. An open home is a sign of an open heart and a loving, sacrificial, serving spirit.

"In my work as a church shepherd, I have found that the home is one of the most important tools for reaching and caring for people. Although the shepherd's ministry of hospitality may seem like a small thing, it has great impact on people. If you doubt this, ask those to whom a shepherd has shown hospitality. Invariably they will say that it is one of the most important, pleasant, and memorable aspects of the shepherd's ministry. In His own mysterious ways, God works through the guest-host relationship to encourage and instruct His people. If the local church's shepherds are inhospitable, the local church will be inhospitable. So we must never underestimate the power of hospitality in ministering to people's needs. Those who love hospitality love people and are concerned about them."

Alexander Strauch[2]

8. The free, open exercise of hospitality is required of elders. Carefully consider the New Testament teaching on hospitality (pp. 194, 195)

    a. What do the following verses teach about hospitality?

    Rom. 12:10, 13

    1 Peter 4:8-10

    Heb. 13:1, 2

b.   Why is hospitality required of church elders?

c.   What does this requirement reveal about the nature of the local church?

ASSIGNMENT:

The biblical importance of hospitality is explained in Alexander Strauch's booklet, *The Hospitality Commands: Building Loving Christian Community, Building Bridges to Friends and Neighbors.* In addition, Edith Schaeffer's *L'Abri* (French for shelter) is an inspiring book on the power of hospitality in demonstrating the love of Christ and the reality of the gospel.

9.   Define the following elder qualifications:

a.   Loving what is good:

b.   Just:

c.   Devout:

LESSON 9

10. Paul was very specific in requiring that elders be able to teach the Word. He describes this elder qualification as **"holding fast the faithful word which is in accordance with the teaching."**

    a. What is the meaning of this qualification (see pp. 79, 80, 195)?

    b. According to Titus 1:10-16, why does Paul insist that this qualification is particularly necessary for an elder on the Island of Crete?

11. Elders are expected to prepare for exhorting the believers and refuting false teachers.

    a. What does being prepared **"to exhort in sound doctrine"** imply about preparation for eldership?

    b. What does being prepared **"to refute"** false teachers imply about preparation for eldership?

ASSIGNMENTS:

To prepare for defending the gospel against false teachers, make it your goal over the next several years to master the books of Romans and Galatians. These books deal with the heart of the gospel and Christian living. They are the centerpiece books of the New Testament and of biblical theology. It is prudent to use a number of sound commentaries on Romans and Galatians and to listen to the expository preaching of several teachers on them. When you are able, confirm your mastery of Romans and Galatians by teaching them to others.

12. Evaluate yourself in each of the following qualifications, specified in Titus 1:6-9. Ask your wife or a close friend to make an independent evaluation of you as well.

    a. Not self-willed: a gentle, forbearing man:

Needs Improvement

_____7_____6_____5_____4_____3_____2_____1_____

Exemplary   Discredited

    b. Not quick-tempered:

Needs Improvement

_____7_____6_____5_____4_____3_____2_____1_____

Exemplary   Discredited

    c. Loving what is good: a kind, virtuous man:

Needs Improvement

_____7_____6_____5_____4_____3_____2_____1_____

Exemplary   Discredited

    d. Just: a righteous, law-abiding man:

Needs Improvement

_____7_____6_____5_____4_____3_____2_____1_____

Exemplary   Discredited

    e. Devout: a holy man, pleasing to God, loyal to His Word:

Needs Improvement

_____7_____6_____5_____4_____3_____2_____1_____

Exemplary   Discredited

    f. Self-controlled: a man controlled by the Holy Spirit:

Needs Improvement

_____7_____6_____5_____4_____3_____2_____1_____

Exemplary   Discredited

    g. Committed to the Word of God: a man who holds fast the trustworthy Word:

Needs Improvement

_____7_____6_____5_____4_____3_____2_____1_____

Exemplary   Discredited

h. A man who is able to exhort in sound doctrine:

Needs Improvement

_____7_____6_____5_____4_____3_____2_____1_____
Exemplary   Discredited

i. A man who is able to reprove and refute those who contradict sound doctrine:

Needs Improvement

_____7_____6_____5_____4_____3_____2_____1_____
Exemplary   Discredited

APPOINTMENT, ORDINATION, AND CLERGY

"Appoint elders in every city."   Titus 1:5c

> Read pages 277-289. Review pages 111-114.

13. List several key reasons why it is wise to avoid using the term "ordination" in reference to elder appointment.

a.

b.

c.

d.

14. Why is official, public installation of the elder important both to the church and to its officers?

    a.   The church:

    b.   The church's officers:

15. What reasons support the assertion that the clergy-laity division among the people of God is not biblical?

    a.

    b.

    c.

    d.

e.

 16. From your own study and experience, what do you think is the single, most damaging consequence of the clergy-laity division for the local church? Explain your answer.

Scripture Memory Assignment:

"For this reason I left you in Crete, that you would set in order what remains and appoint elders in every city as I directed you, namely, if any man is above reproach, the husband of one wife, having children who believe, not accused of dissipation or rebellion. For the overseer must be above reproach as God's steward, not self-willed, not quick-tempered, not addicted to wine, not pugnacious, not fond of sordid gain, but hospitable, loving what is good, sensible, just, devout, self-controlled, holding fast the faithful word which is in accordance with the teaching, so that he will be able both to exhort in sound doctrine and to refute those who contradict."
Titus 1:5-9

---

[1] D. E. Hoste, *If I Am to Lead* (London: Overseas Missionary Fellowship, 1968), pp. 16, 17.
[2] Alexander Strauch, *The Hospitality Commands* (Littleton: Lewis and Roth, 1993), pp. 43, 44.

LESSON 10

SHEPHERD GOD'S FLOCK IN GOD'S WAY

LESSON OVERVIEW

In lesson 10, Peter's farewell exhortations to the elders of northwestern Asia Minor in 1 Peter 5:1-3 are considered. We examine the urgent apostolic imperative for elders to shepherd God's flock, that is, to be all that shepherds should be to the flock. This lesson will help you think practically about your time commitment to the shepherding task and your personal contribution to the shepherding team.

Furthermore, this passage is an urgent call for pastor elders to shepherd the flock in a distinctly Christlike way–willingly, eagerly, and as godly models of Christ–not as authoritarian tyrants or hirelings. Christian elders are to be loving, servant leaders.

SHEPHERD GOD'S FLOCK

"Therefore, I exhort the elders among you, as your fellow elder and witness of the sufferings of Christ, and a partaker also of the glory that is to be revealed, shepherd the flock of God among you." 1 Peter 5:1, *2a*

Review pages 9-31. Read pages 239-244.

1.   What is Peter's purpose in calling himself a "fellow elder" in 1 Peter 5:1?

2. How does the verb "shepherd" (v. 2, p. 149) help you differentiate between the concept of elders that most people and churches have today (see pp. 9-17) and the New Testament concept?

a. The contemporary view of elders is:

Administrative leaders / Church managers

b. The New Testament view of elders is:

servant leader, helping promote spiritual growth by example first

3. Understanding the sense of urgency for the elders' task:

a. A deep sense of urgency pervades Peter's charge to the Asian elders. According to the entire letter of 1 Peter, what is the cause of this urgency?

b. Do you personally feel a sense of urgency about shepherding God's flock? Why?

4. The shepherding task:

a. Describe six responsibilities involved in the shepherding task (pp. 16-31).

1 *Protecting the flock*

2 *Feeding the flock*

3 Leading the Flock

4 Caring for the Practical Needs

5 Love for the flock

6 Hard Work

b. Which aspects of the shepherding task are you best gifted to perform?

1 Protecting, 3 Feeding, 2 Leading

c. Which aspects of the shepherding task are you weakest at performing, or least interested in? Caring for practical needs

d. What are you doing, or could you do, to improve your weak areas of shepherding?

should I focus on improving weak areas or excel in gifts.

e. Write the action plan to which you and your mentoring elder have agreed.

5. The character traits of a good shepherd:

a. What were the character traits of a good Palestinian shepherd (pp. 16, 17, 149, and John 10:1-18)?

intimacy, tenderness, concern, skill, hardwork, suffering, love

b. In which of these character traits are you strongest?

concern, tenderness

c. In which are you weakest? intimacy/suffering

d. In light of your strong character traits, what positive contributions will you be able to make to the shepherding team?

to aid in people feeling more connected to the church & the leaders

Peter charges the elders to shepherd the flock, which is a time-consuming task. Neil Summerton clearly describes the practical reality of shepherding:

> The demands of personal and group prayer, of meeting in oversight, of preparation for teaching, of pastoral visitation, and of giving necessary leadership and guidance to congregational activities are inevitably very great. A particular individual may have the character and gifts, and even the inclination, to be an elder, *but may not have the time* (italics added).[1]

 So, as a prospective elder, you must honestly ask yourself, *Do I have the time to help shepherd God's flock?*

As a busy person, you must acquire effective management skills. We highly recommend reading Charles H. Hummel's short booklet, *The Tyranny of the Urgent.* Hummel reminds us of the principle that the busier we are and the more responsibilities we manage, the more important it is to take time regularly to plan and evaluate our schedule and priorities:

> Ironically, the busier you get the more you need this time of inventory, but the less you seem to be able to take it. You become like the fanatic, who, when unsure of his direction, doubles his speed. And frenetic service for God can become an escape from God. But when you prayerfully take inventory and plan your days, it provides fresh perspective on your work.[2]

> We live in constant tension between the urgent and the important. The problem is that the important task rarely must be done today, or even this week. Extra hours of prayer and Bible study, a visit with that non-Christian friend, careful study of an important book: these projects can wait. But the urgent tasks call for instant action–endless demands pressure every hour and day.[3]

ASSIGNMENT:

Although you are not yet an elder, carefully consider how you would spend the time you have available for serving as a shepherd elder. Be very specific. Write out a monthly schedule that realistically represents the time you would spend in specific pastoral work and personal, spiritual preparation. For example: two nights for two hours a week studying Scripture at home in preparation for teaching a class, one night a week for three hours visiting members in their homes or counseling, one night a week for two hours in small group Bible study, two nights a month at elders' meetings for three hours, one night a week for two hours for corporate prayer, etc. Before you finalize your chart, talk over your time commitments with your wife and children as well as your mentor.

SUNDAY	MONDAY	TUESDAY	WEDNESDAY	THURSDAY	FRIDAY	SATURDAY

6. What activities and responsibilities in your life need adjustment in order to allow the time needed for your work as a member of the shepherding team? Discuss these adjustments with your wife first, then your mentor.

SHEPHERD GOD'S FLOCK IN GOD'S WAY

"Shepherd the flock of God among you, exercising oversight not under compulsion, but voluntarily, according to the will of God; and not for sordid gain, but with eagerness; nor yet as lording it over those allotted to your charge, but proving to be examples to the flock."   1 Peter 5:2, 3

LESSON 10

Read pages 244-248. Review pages 85-98.

7. Why is Peter deeply concerned about the attitudes and motives of those who lead God's flock?

proving to be examples to the flock

8. Elders must serve **"not under compulsion"**:

a. In 1 Peter 5:2, what does Peter mean by the term *compulsion*?

voluntarily, ~~~~ according to God's will

b. Why does Peter prohibit a man from serving as an elder if he serves under compulsion?

being felt forced vs. acting on God's will

c. What is God's standard for the motives of those who oversee His flock, and why?

- Eager, Being examples, Holy
- That they will glorify God as they observe our good deeds

"What is the essential difference between spurious and true Christian leadership? When a man, in virtue of . . . an official position in the church, demands the obedience of another, irrespective of the latter's reason and conscience, this is the spirit of tyranny. When, on the other hand, by the exercise of tact and sympathy, by prayer, spiritual power and sound wisdom, one Christian worker is able to influence and enlighten another, so that the latter, through the medium of his own reason and conscience, is led to alter one course and adopt another, this is true spiritual leadership."

D. E. Hoste[4]

9. *Eagerness* is a wonderful quality. How would you describe an elder who *eagerly* shepherds God's flock?

Anxious to help, ready, looking for Gods activity in peoples lives & eager to "jump-in".

> "When we consider Paul's example and that of our Lord's, we must agree that biblical elders do not dictate, they direct. True elders do not command the consciences of their brethren, but appeal to their brethren to faithfully follow God's Word. Out of love, true elders suffer and bear the brunt of difficult people and problems so that the lambs are not bruised. They bear the misunderstanding and sins of others so that the assembly may live in peace. They lose sleep so that others may rest. They make great personal sacrifices of time and energy for the welfare of others. They see themselves as men under authority. They depend on God for wisdom and help, not on their own power and cleverness. They face the false teachers' fierce attacks. They guard the community's liberty and freedom in Christ so that the saints are encouraged to develop their gifts, to mature, and to serve one another."
>
> Alexander Strauch[5]

10. An authoritarian style of church leadership is sternly prohibited by Christ and His apostles (Matt. 18:4; 20:20-28; 1 Peter 1:22; 2:16; 3:8-11; 4:8; 5:5, 6; 2 Tim. 2:24, 25). Yet the Lord requires that church leaders diligently lead the church (Rom. 12:8; 1 Tim. 5:17). Thus, pastor elders are to lead diligently and effectively, but not in an authoritarian manner. After reading chapter 5, "Servant Leadership" (pp. 85-98, 114), list the chief distinctives of both the authoritarian style of church leadership, which Christ denounces, and the diligent, servant style of church leadership.

a. Marks of an authoritarian leadership style:

Pride, Selfish, devisions, power-struggles, wounded feelings

b. Marks of a diligent, servant leadership style:

Gentle, Humble, Servants, Sacrificial, Service, Suffering

11. As you read the following list of the marks of an unhealthy, controlling leader, check your own leadership style for any unhealthy tendencies that need prayer and accountability.

    __   Self-centered and self-willed

    __   Shuns genuine, peer accountability

    __   Must control church finances

    __   Overly concerned with externals and appearances

    __   Sees all issues as black and white, operates only in extremes, and views people as for or against himself

    __   Threatened by legitimate change or differences

    __   A negative, unaccepting mentality; a closed mind

    __   Hypercritical of others, but unable to see his own glaring sins, errors, and faults

    __   Fearful of competent, gifted people

    __   Cannot delegate genuine authority or significant positions to others

    __   Lacks balance

    __   Manipulates people

    __   Seeks spotlight, recognition

12. List some of Paul's leadership characteristics (pp. 93-95).

13. Why have Christ's teachings on love, humility, and servanthood been so hard for churches and church leaders to practice?

14. How would you apply the following quotation by Francis A. Schaeffer to Peter's phrase "those allotted to your charge"?

"As there are no little people in God's sight, so there are no little places. To be wholly committed to God in the place where God wants him–this is the creature glorified . . . . Nowhere more than in America are Christians caught in the twentieth-century syndrome of size. Size will show success. If I am consecrated, there will necessarily be large quantities of people, dollars, etc. This is not so. Not only does God not say that size and spiritual power go together, but he even reverses this (especially in the teaching of Jesus) and tells us to be deliberately careful not to choose a place too big for us. We all tend to emphasize big works and big places, but all such emphasis is of the flesh. To think in such terms is simply to hearken back to the old, unconverted, egoist, self-centered *Me*. This attitude, taken from the world, is more dangerous to the Christian than fleshly amusement or practice. It is the flesh."

Francis A. Schaeffer[6]

a. Success in the flock is *not* tied to size or money

b. God sees success as: God's people wholly committed to Him

SCRIPTURE MEMORY ASSIGNMENT:

"Therefore, I exhort the elders among you, as your fellow elder and witness of the sufferings of Christ, and a partaker also of the glory that is to be revealed, shepherd the flock of God among you, exercising oversight not under compulsion, but voluntarily, according to the will of God; and not for sordid gain, but with eagerness; nor yet as lording it over those allotted to your charge, but proving to be examples to the flock."   1 Peter 5:1-3

---

[1] Neil Summerton, *A Noble Task: Eldership and Ministry in the Local Church*, 2nd ed. (Carlisle: Paternoster, 1994), p. 27.

[2] Charles H. Hummel, *Tyranny of the Urgent* (Downers Grove: InterVarsity, 1967), p. 14.

[3] Ibid., p. 5.

[4] D. E. Hoste, *If I Am to Lead* (London: Overseas Missionary Fellowship, 1968), p. 7.

[5] Alexander Strauch, *Biblical Eldership: An Urgent Call to Restore Biblical Church Leadership* (Littleton: Lewis and Roth, 1995), p. 98.

[6] Francis A. Schaeffer, *No Little People* (Downers Grove: InterVarsity, 1974), p. 18.

LESSON 11

CARING FOR THE POOR
PRAYING FOR THE SICK

LESSON OVERVIEW

Lesson 11 addresses the elders' attitude toward the poor and needy, and the character qualities necessary in the men who administer the church's charitable funds. The second half of the lesson deals with the elders' responsibility to the sick, as described in James 5:14, 15. To be a Christlike shepherd, the elder must be compassionate toward those who suffer. In ministering to the sick, the pastor elder must be a man of faith, prayer, and wise counsel.

CARING FOR THE POOR

"And in the proportion that any of the disciples [in Antioch] had means, each of them determined to send a contribution for the relief of the brethren living in Judea. And this they did, sending it in charge of Barnabas and Saul to the elders."
                                                                                    Acts 11:29, 30

"'In everything I showed you that by working hard in this manner you must help the weak and remember the words of the Lord Jesus, that He Himself said, "It is more blessed to give than to receive."'"
                                                                                    Acts 20:35

Review pages 156-159.

The first time Luke mentions the Jewish Christian elders (Acts 11:27-30, p. 124), giving to the needy is the subject. The elders in Jerusalem received an offering from the Christians in Antioch for the relief of the destitute saints in Judea. Stressing the significance of our responsibility to the poor, the eighteenth-century American pastor-theologian, Jonathan Edwards (1703-1758), wrote: "I know of scarce any duty which is so much insisted on, so pressed and urged upon us, both in the Old Testament and New, as this duty of charity to the poor."[1] The following Old Testament passages reveal the explicit directions given to Israel concerning the poor and needy:

Deut. 15:7-10 "If there is a poor man with you, one of your brothers, in any of your towns in your land which the Lord your God is giving you, you shall not harden your heart, nor close your hand from your poor brother; but you shall freely open your hand to him, and shall generously lend him sufficient for his need in whatever he lacks. Beware that there is no base thought in your heart, saying, 'The seventh year, the year of remission, is near,' and your eye is hostile toward your poor brother, and you give him nothing; then he may cry to the Lord against you, and it will be a sin in you. You shall generously give to him, and your heart shall not be grieved when you give to him, because for this thing the Lord your God will bless you in all your work and in all your undertakings."

Prov. 14:31 He who oppresses the poor reproaches his Maker, but he who is gracious to the needy honors Him.

Prov. 19:17 He who is gracious to a poor man lends to the Lord, and He will repay him for his good deed.

Prov. 21:13 He who shuts his ear to the cry of the poor will also cry himself and not be answered.

Prov. 22:9 He who is generous will be blessed, for he gives some of his food to the poor.

Prov. 29:7 The righteous is concerned for the rights of the poor, the wicked does not understand such concern.

This compassion for the poor was also demonstrated by the New Testament church.

Acts 4:34, 35 For there was not a needy person among them, for all who were owners of land or houses would sell them and bring the proceeds of the sales and lay them at the apostles' feet, and they would be distributed to each as any had need.

Eph. 4:28 He who steals must steal no longer; but rather he must labor, performing with his own hands what is good, so that he will have something to share with one who has need.

Gal. 2:10 They [James and John] only asked us [Paul and Barnabas] to remember the poor—the very thing I [Paul] also was eager to do.

James 1:27a Pure and undefiled religion in the sight of our God and Father is this: to visit orphans and widows in their distress.

1 John 3:17 But whoever has the world's goods, and sees his brother in need and closes his heart against him, how does the love of God abide in him?

1.   In light of these passages, who is your brother?

2. Write down the *wrong attitudes or actions* toward the poor brother that you see in these passages.

a. holding back from the poor as the 7th yr. approaches (Remission)

b. Oppressing the poor Reproaches the maker

c. shuts his ears to the poor

d. the wicked does not have concern for the poor

e.

3. What five *positive attitudes or actions* are we to have toward the brother who is in need?

a. the generous will be blessed

b. the righteous are concerned for the poor

c. all would sell all they had & it was sold / distributed

d. Paul only asked us to remember the poor.

e. love of God = helps people in need

4. List the consequences to us of our treatment of our poor brothers.

    a. Consequences of improper treatment:

    prayers not answered
    no blessings
    God shuts his ears —

    b. Consequences of proper treatment:

    Blessing

5. Paul instructs the Ephesian elders and, therefore, all shepherd elders, to work hard and share their earnings with poor and needy brothers. Compare Galatians 2:10 and 1 Timothy 3:3*b*.

    Acts 20:34, 35 "You [elders] yourselves know that these [Paul's] hands ministered to my own needs and to the men who were with me. In everything I showed you that by working hard in this manner you must help the weak and remember the words of the Lord Jesus, that He Himself said, 'It is more blessed to give than to receive.'"

    a. Why is it important to the local church that its elders model the practices of hard work and benevolence?

    — working hard allows us to give more
    — it demonstrates a good work ethic
        "   "   "   benevolence
    ① "Eager" to remember the poor

    b. What does leadership in this area imply about the elder's standard of living?

    ② Not a lover of money
        ↳ not attached to material wealth/things

6. The qualifications of and standards for an elder are listed below.

1 Timothy 3:2-7	**Titus 1:6-9**	**1 Peter 5:1-3**
1. Above reproach	1. Above reproach	1. Not shepherding under compulsion, but voluntarily
2. The husband of one wife	2. The husband of one wife	2. Not shepherding for sordid gain, but with eagerness
3. Temperate [self-controlled, balanced]	3. Having children who believe	3. Not lording it over the flock, but proving to be an example
4. Prudent [sensible, good judgment]	4. Not self-willed	
5. Respectable [well-behaved, virtuous]	5. Not quick-tempered	
6. Hospitable	6. Not addicted to wine	
7. Able to teach	7. Not pugnacious	
8. Not addicted to wine	8. Not fond of sordid gain	
9. Not pugnacious [not belligerent]	9. Hospitable	
10. Gentle [forbearing]	10. Lover of what is good [kind, virtuous]	
11. Peaceable [uncontentious]	11. Sensible [see prudent]	
12. Free from the love of money	12. Just [righteous conduct, law-abiding]	
13. Manages his household well	13. Devout [holy, pleasing to God, loyal to His Word]	
14. Not a new convert	14. Self-controlled	
15. A good reputation with those outside the church	15. Holds fast the faithful [trustworthy NIV] Word, both to exhort and to refute	

Those who distribute contributions for the needy and/or receive financial support for the work of ministry are vulnerable to temptation and criticism. List below the requisite qualities for the man who handles the church's benevolence funds. Beside each quality, point out the result: either how the elder should be viewed, or how he should behave.

a. Example: ***Above reproach, respectable:*** *Trusted by the congregation*

b. Prudent / Good Judgement   Sensible in handling it

      "What is mine, is yours"

c. Hospitable   —

d. Free from love of money

e. Not fond of sordid gain

f. Just / Righteous — makes right decisions

g. Devout

h.

7. In Acts 6, the apostles ask the church to choose men (the first deacons or the precursors of deacons) to be responsible for the distribution of food so that the Twelve could devote their attention to the ministry of the Word.

a. Is it proper for present-day elders to delegate some or all of their responsibility to the poor to a deacon board?

* Need to watch over to verify that it continues & is done appropriately
*

b. What advantage would such delegation have for both the elders and the poor?

Frees the elders to teach the Word

8. Describe improper delegation (poor leadership by the elders) in the overseeing of care for the needy.

lack of demonstrating

9.   Study Matthew 25:34-40. Explain how this passage should revolutionize your thinking about helping poor, needy believers.

Hungrey – you fed me, thirsty give to drink,
Stranger – invited in
Clothe those who need clothes
Sick or (in prison – Visit me)

when you do it to the least of my brothers – you did it for me.

PRAYING FOR THE SICK

"Is anyone among you suffering? Then he must pray. Is anyone cheerful? He is to sing praises. Is anyone among you sick? Then he must call for the elders of the church and they are to pray over him, anointing him with oil in the name of the Lord; and the prayer offered in faith will restore the one who is sick, and the Lord will raise him up, and if he has committed sins, they will be forgiven him. Therefore, confess your sins to one another, and pray for one another so that you may be healed. The effective prayer of a righteous man can accomplish much."   James 5:13-16

Review pages 29-31. Read pages 253-263.

Too often we men are not as compassionate as we should be toward those who suffer or are sick. We are like Job's friends, insensitive doctors of the soul. Our supreme model and mentor, however, is the Lord Jesus Christ. He was full of compassion for the sick and weak. The Presbyterian scholar, B. B. Warfield, wrote a significant article entitled, "On the Emotional Life of our Lord." Warfield states that compassion is the chief emotion expressed by our Lord:

> The emotion which we should naturally expect to find most frequently attributed to that Jesus whose whole life was a mission of mercy, and whose ministry was so marked by deeds of beneficence that it was summed up in the memory of his followers as a going through the land "doing good" (Acts 11:48), is no doubt "compassion." In point of fact, this is the emotion which is most frequently attributed to him.[2]

A lack of compassion is actually a lack of love. Warfield says that the fountain-spring of Christ's compassion was His love:

> Jesus' prime characteristic was love, and love is the foundation of compassion . . . . It is characteristic of John's Gospel that it goes with simple directness always to the bottom of things. Love lies at the bottom of compassion. And love is attributed to Jesus only once in the Synoptics, but compassion often; while with John the contrary is true–compassion is attributed to Jesus not even once, but love often. This love is commonly the love of compassion.[3]

LESSON 11

Quoting from A. W. Tozer's biography of Robert Jaffrey, J. Oswald Sanders infers that all great spiritual leaders are characterized by compassion and love for people:

> In his biography of Robert A. Jaffrey, who played a major part in opening Vietnam to the gospel, A. W. Tozer pointed out that in one respect all spiritual leaders have been alike. They have all had large hearts. "Nothing can take the place of affection. Those who have it in generous measure have a magic power over men. Intellect will not do. Bible knowledge is not enough. Robert Jaffrey loved people for their own sakes. He was happy in the presence of human beings, whatever their race and colour."[4]

A Christlike shepherd, then, must be a man of love and compassion.

10. Using your concordance, look under the heading "compassion." Spell out for whom Jesus actually felt compassion.

   a. *compassion, before advice / forgiveness of debts,*

   b. Choose, from the categories of people you listed above, those for whom you feel the most compassion. Why is this?

11. Which three elder qualifications most completely represent the concept of compassion or love? Explain why.

   a. *Hospitable*

   b. *Free from the love of money*

   c. *Prudent*

12. Shepherding the flock of God is a profoundly spiritual work that demands Spirit-filled leaders (Acts 6:3). What does James indicate must be true of elders if they are to participate in an effective ministry to the sick (James 5:13-16)?

13. How would you counsel someone who asks why he or she hasn't been healed after fervent, believing prayer? What Scripture texts would you use?

14. How would you counsel a sick person who asks if his or her sickness is the result of personal sin? What Scripture texts would you use?

15. What are the two main, contending views put forth today concerning application of oil to the sick by the elders? Indicate the view you support.

    a.

    b.

    c.   Explain why you hold the position you do.

16. What are some practical benefits for both the sick person and the elders of praying in the sick person's presence (at his bedside) rather than praying at a distance, in a church building?

ASSIGNMENTS:

Write a short list of specific, practical guidelines that will help you be effective when you visit the sick, whether they are at home or in the hospital. Ask your elders for their ideas, practices, and procedures. List some key Scripture references to read to the sick. Ask your elders to include you the next time they are called to pray for the sick so that you can learn how to minister to the sick. When our congregation's elders are called to a home or hospital to pray for a sick person, these are specific aspects of our practice:

- We take songbooks along and sing appropriate songs. This establishes a good atmosphere for prayer and seeking the Lord's intervention.

- Each elder shares from the Word (see questions **13.** and **14.**) and gives encouragement and counsel to the one who is sick and his or her family, if present. At this time, one of the elders lovingly asks about the person's relationship to the Lord and if there is unconfessed sin. We have not experienced any adverse reaction to this question. Most sick people who call for the elders are willing to face honestly their relationship to the Lord.

- One of the elders explains the significance of the oil (see question **15.**) and applies oil to the sick person.

- We all kneel and pray. Each elder prays at least once.

- While they pray, one or two of the elders will lay hands on or hold the hand of the person who is sick, communicating our love and affection.

SCRIPTURE MEMORY ASSIGNMENT:

"Is anyone among you sick? Then he must call for the elders of the church and they are to pray over him, anointing him with oil in the name of the Lord; and the prayer offered in faith will restore the one who is sick, and the Lord will raise him up, and if he has committed sins, they will be forgiven him. Therefore, confess your sins to one another, and pray for one another so that you may be healed. The effective prayer of a righteous man can accomplish much." James 5:14-16

---

[1] Jonathan Edwards, *The Works of Jonathan Edwards*, 2 Vols. (1834; repr. Edinburgh: The Banner of Truth Trust, 1974), 2:164.

[2] B. B. Warfield, "On the Emotional Life of Our Lord," in *The Person and Work of Christ* (Philadelphia: Presbyterian and Reformed, 1950), p. 104.

[3] Ibid., p. 101.

[4] J. Oswald Sanders, *Spiritual Leadership* (Chicago: Moody, 1980), p. 90.

LESSON 12

SPIRITUAL WATCHMEN
SUBMISSION TO AUTHORITY
MALE LEADERSHIP

LESSON OVERVIEW

The final lesson explores Hebrews 13:17. We discuss the institutional church model versus the community church model, and the joys and heartaches of leading God's people. In addition, the subject of submission to church elders, a matter of great disdain to modern man, is studied.

The lesson also reviews chapter 3 of *Biblical Eldership*, "Male Leadership." This is not only an issue related to God's plan for male-female relationships in the home and church, but is an issue of biblical integrity and authority that is of utmost importance to the Lord's people.

SPIRITUAL WATCHMEN

"Obey your leaders and submit to them, for they keep watch over your souls as those who will give an account. Let them do this with joy and not with grief, for this would be unprofitable for you."

Hebrews 13:17

Read pages 265-273.

In his description of the differences between the institutional church model and the community church model, Stephen B. Clark writes:

> In most churches in the Western world, the institutional elements predominate over communal elements. The reverse was true among the early Christians. . . . In a communal grouping like that of the early Christians, the overall leadership of the community governed the people. The heads of the Christian communities functioned in a way similar to fathers in a family; they did not treat the community members like children, but they did lead and direct them personally. They governed (cared for) the people. They taught them and watched over their lives. When members

of the community were in need, the elders saw that the need was met. When the lives of the community members did not conform to the Lord's way of life, the heads would personally discuss the issue with those members. If a major transgression occurred, the elders would discipline the person. They governed and led the people, not the institution.

By contrast, the leaders of most modern churches concern themselves more directly with the institution than with the people, and their leadership consists primarily of administration, decision-making, and opinion-forming. The people's lives are a private matter. The leader will counsel someone upon request. The leader will run a program for those who want something enough to sign up and participate. The leader thus provides services for some individuals when they express a personal interest. The authority of church leaders extends over the institution–the common activities–but not the lives of the church members. The leaders can influence the direction of their members' lives through educational activities, but their primary authoritative functions are either administrative or policy-making for the institution (decision-making about budgets, hiring personnel, types of programs to use, etc.)[1].

1. Show that the community concept of church life is the only valid understanding of Hebrews 13:17.

2. This passage contains two important Greek words that are essential to a proper understanding of biblical eldership.

    a. What is the meaning of the Greek term *agryneō* in this context?

    b. What is the meaning of *psychē* in this context?

    c. What do you learn about the significance of the elders' work from these two terms?

3. How will the fact that elders must give an account of their stewardship to the Lord affect your efforts as a spiritual caregiver and leader?

4. What aspects of shepherding bring the greatest joy to the elder's heart?

"Something has already been said regarding the character of the pastor. In Paul's eyes he must be a patient and gentle teacher who is firmly committed to the truth. But [Paul's] troubles with the church at Corinth caused him to reveal a much deeper side to pastoral life than this. *Pastoral life can be painful and costly and [no one] can be more vulnerable to the wounds inflicted by others than the true pastor.*

"[Paul] reveals in 2 Corinthians how some of his own children had criticized him for being fickle (1:15-17), speaking with a double tongue (1:13; 10:1, 10), of lacking credentials (3:1), of being untrustworthy with money (8:20, 21), of acting in a worldly fashion (10:2), of being proud and deceitful (10:8; 12:16), of not being an original apostle (11:5) and of lacking dignity (11:7). The misunderstandings had led to a rupture in relationships, with the Corinthians not communicating with Paul in any meaningful way (7:2). It was all the harder because it was a family relationship which was disrupted and because Paul took such delight in them (12:14, 15; 7:3, 4). It was also hard because it came on top of all his other pressures (11:22-28). What is more, he was innocent. The strife had been stirred up by impostors (11:13), who in contrast to Paul had no legitimate place in the church at Corinth (10:13)" (italics added).

Derek J. Tidball[2]

The emotional stresses and heavy burdens of caring for the spiritual welfare of people can break a man's health and his resolve to do the work. It is not the hard work or long hours that defeat a man; it is the emotional and spiritual stress that crushes a man's spirit. To be specific, constant fighting among believers, complaints, unbelief, and disobedience ultimately wear down a Christian elder.

If you are inexperienced in the shepherding ministry, the Scripture references that follow will inform you of the harsh realities of working with people. Even the mighty Moses was broken by the people's incessant complaining and unbelief (Num. 11:15). Unrealistic or romantic ideas of Christian ministry eventually lead to disillusionment and discouragement.

5. Based on the passages below, list the major problems with the people and their attitudes that elders can expect to face when leading God's people.

Ex. 14:10-12 As Pharaoh drew near, the sons of Israel looked, and behold, the Egyptians were marching after them, and they became very frightened; so the sons of Israel cried out to the Lord. Then they said to Moses, "Is it because there were no graves in Egypt that you have taken us away to die in the wilderness? Why have you dealt with us in this way, bringing us out of Egypt? Is this not the word that we spoke to you in Egypt, saying, 'Leave us alone that we may serve the Egyptians?' For it would have been better for us to serve the Egyptians than to die in the wilderness."

Num. 11:4-6, 10-15 The rabble who were among them had greedy desires; and also the sons of Israel wept again and said, "Who will give us meat to eat? We remember the fish which we used to eat free in Egypt, the cucumbers and the melons and the leeks and the onions and the garlic, but now our appetite is gone. There is nothing at all to look at except this manna."

Now Moses heard the people weeping throughout their families, each man at the doorway of his tent; and the anger of the Lord was kindled greatly, and Moses was displeased. So Moses said to the Lord, "Why have You been so hard on Your servant? And why have I not found favor in Your sight, that you have laid the burden of all this people on me? Was it I who conceived all this people? Was it I who brought them forth, that You should say to me, 'Carry them in your bosom as a nurse carries a nursing infant, to the land which You swore to their fathers?' Where am I to get meat to give to all this people? For they weep before me, saying, 'Give us meat that we may eat!' I alone am not able to carry all this people, because it is too burdensome for me. So if You are going to deal thus with me, please kill me at once, if I have found favor in Your sight, and do not let me see my wretchedness."

Num. 12:1-3, 5, 8b Then Miriam and Aaron [Moses' sister and brother] spoke against Moses because of the Cushite woman whom he had married . . . and they said, "Has the Lord indeed spoken only through Moses? Has He not spoken through us as well?" And the Lord heard it. (Now the man Moses was very humble, more than any man who was on the face of the earth.) . . . Then the Lord came down in a pillar of cloud and stood at the doorway of the tent, and He called Aaron and Miriam. When they had both come forward, . . . [He said] "Why then were you not afraid to speak against My servant, against Moses?"

Num. 14:1-4 Then all the congregation lifted up their voices and cried, and the people wept that night. All the sons of Israel grumbled against Moses and Aaron; and the whole congregation said to them, "Would that we had died in the land of Egypt! Or would that we had died in this wilderness! Why is the Lord bringing us into this land, to fall by the sword? Our wives and our little ones will become plunder; would it not be better for us to return to Egypt?" So they said to one another, "Let us appoint a leader and return to Egypt."

Num. 16:1-4, 7*b***, 9, 12-14** Now Korah . . . with Dathan and Abiram . . . rose up before Moses, together with . . . two hundred and fifty leaders of the congregation, chosen in the assembly, men of renown. They assembled together against Moses and Aaron, and said to them, "You have gone far enough, for all the congregation are holy, every one of them, and the Lord is in their midst; so why do you exalt yourselves above the assembly of the Lord?" When Moses heard this, he fell on his face. . . . [He said] "You have gone far enough, you sons of Levi! . . . Is it not enough for you that the God of Israel has separated you from the rest of the congregation of Israel, to bring you near to Himself, to do the service of the tabernacle of the Lord, and to stand before the congregation to minister to them?"

Then Moses sent a summons to Dathan and Abiram, the sons of Eliab; but they said, "We will not come up. Is it not enough that you have brought us up out of a land flowing with milk and honey to have us die in the wilderness, but you would also lord it over us? Indeed, you have not brought us into a land flowing with milk and honey, nor have you given us an inheritance of fields and vineyards. Would you put out the eyes of these men? We will not come up!"

Num. 21:4, 5 Then they set out from Mount Hor by the way of the Red Sea, to go around the land of Edom; and the people became impatient because of the journey. The people spoke against God and Moses, "Why have you brought us up out of Egypt to die in the wilderness? For there is no food and no water, and we loathe this miserable food."

Deut. 1:42, 43 "And the Lord said to me [Moses], 'Say to them, "Do not go up nor fight, for I am not among you; otherwise you will be defeated before your enemies."' So I spoke to you, but you would not listen. Instead you rebelled against the command of the Lord, and acted presumptuously and went up into the hill country."

Judg. 8:34, 35 Thus the sons of Israel did not remember the Lord their God, who had delivered them from the hands of all their enemies on every side; nor did they show kindness to the household of Jerubbaal (that is, Gideon), in accord with all the good that he had done to Israel.

1 Sam. 8:19, 20 Nevertheless, the people refused to listen to the voice of Samuel, and they said, "No, but there shall be a king over us, that we also may be like all the nations, that our king may judge us and go out before us and fight our battles."

1 Sam. 30:6 Moreover David was greatly distressed because the people spoke of stoning him, for all the people were embittered, each one because of his sons and his daughters. But David strengthened himself in the Lord his God.

2 Sam. 17:1-4 Furthermore, Ahithophel [one of David's chief counselors] said to Absalom [David's son], "Please let me choose 12,000 men that I may arise and pursue David tonight. I will come upon him while he is weary and exhausted and will terrify him so that all the people who are with him will flee. Then I will strike down the king alone, and I will bring back all the people to you. The return of everyone depends on the man you seek; then all the people shall be at peace." So the plan pleased Absalom and all the elders of Israel.

2 Chron. 36:15, 16 The Lord, the God of their fathers, sent word to them again and again by His messengers, because He had compassion on His people and on His dwelling place; but they continually mocked the messengers of God, despised His words and scoffed at His prophets, until the wrath of the Lord arose against His people, until there was no remedy.

Matt. 26:56b Then all the disciples left Him and fled.

1 Cor. 4:18 Now some have become arrogant, as though I were not coming to you.

2 Cor. 11:20, 21 For you tolerate it if anyone enslaves you, anyone devours you, anyone takes advantage of you, anyone exalts himself, anyone hits you in the face. To my shame I must say that we have been weak by comparison. But in whatever respect anyone else is bold–I speak in foolishness–I am just as bold myself.

Gal. 4:16 Have I become your enemy by telling you the truth?

Phil. 1:15, 17 Some, to be sure, are preaching Christ even from envy and strife, but some also from good will; . . . the former proclaim Christ out of selfish ambition rather than from pure motives, thinking to cause me distress in my imprisonment.

2 Tim. 1:15 You are aware of the fact that all who are in Asia turned away from me, among whom are Phygelus and Hermogenes.

6.   From the above list of difficulties, which problems will you find it most difficult to manage and why?

7. From the list of elder qualifications, select those that will help you cope with the hurts and aggravations of working with people. Explain why each qualification will help.

1 Timothy 3:2-7

1. Above reproach
2. The husband of one wife
3. Temperate [self-controlled, balanced]
4. Prudent [sensible, good judgment]
5. Respectable [well-behaved, virtuous]
6. Hospitable
7. Able to teach
8. Not addicted to wine
9. Not pugnacious [not belligerent]
10. Gentle [forbearing]
11. Peaceable [uncontentious]
12. Free from the love of money
13. Manages his household well
14. Not a new convert
15. A good reputation with those outside the church

Titus 1:6-9

1. Above reproach
2. The husband of one wife
3. Having children who believe
4. Not self-willed
5. Not quick-tempered
6. Not addicted to wine
7. Not pugnacious
8. Not fond of sordid gain
9. Hospitable
10. Lover of what is good [kind, virtuous]
11. Sensible [see prudent]
12. Just [righteous conduct, law-abiding]
13. Devout [holy, pleasing to God, loyal to His Word]
14. Self-controlled
15. Holds fast the faithful [trustworthy NIV] Word, both to exhort and to refute

1 Peter 5:1-3

1. Not shepherding under compulsion, but voluntarily
2. Not shepherding for sordid gain, but with eagerness
3. Not lording it over the flock, but proving to be an example

a.

b.

c.

Submission to Authority

"Obey your leaders and submit to them, for they keep watch over your souls as those who will give an account. Let them do this with joy and not with grief, for this would be unprofitable for you."

Hebrews 13:17

Review pages 270-273.

Contemporary personal values and attitudes about authority differ radically from those taught in the Bible. For the most part, modern man rejects the authority of Scripture, denies objective standards of right and wrong, and refuses to accept the moral absolutes of good and evil. As J. I. Packer points out, there is growing contempt for all forms of authority: "Undisguised contempt for restrictions and directions, and truculent defiance which bucks all systems when it is not busy exploiting them, have become almost conventional, and anyone who respects authority stands out as odd."[3]

Describing modern man's contempt for submission, his self-centeredness, and his relativistic thinking, Stephen B. Clark writes:

> Contemporary society, however, does not value personal submission. Rather, it teaches that the ideal, the highest position a human being can attain, is that of personal autonomy. The human being who decides for himself, who is creative, that is, who devises novel opinions or viewpoints, the human being who is "adult," taking the responsibility to make his own decisions–this is the human being who is valued. . . . For the modern mentality, freedom is the ability to set one's own standards, to submit to no person, to chart one's own course.[4]

8.   How have such ideas affected what Christians think about the elders' involvement in their personal lives?

9.   Why is it vitally important to the spiritual development of a believer that he or she obey and submit to the elders of the church?

   a.

   b.

   c.

d.

e.

f.

MALE LEADERSHIP

"Likewise, I want women to adorn themselves with proper clothing, modestly and discreetly, not with braided hair and gold or pearls or costly garments, but rather by means of good works, as is proper for women making a claim to godliness. A woman must quietly receive instruction with entire submissiveness. But I do not allow a woman to teach or exercise authority over a man, but to remain quiet. For it was Adam who was first created, and then Eve. And it was not Adam who was deceived, but the woman being deceived, fell into transgression. But women shall be preserved through the bearing of children if they continue in faith and love and sanctity with self-restraint. It is a trustworthy statement: if any man aspires to the office of overseer, it is a fine work he desires to do. An overseer, then, must be above reproach, the husband of one wife."
1 Timothy 2:9-3:2a

| Review pages 51-66. |

ASSIGNMENT:

Because the concept of male leadership continues to be a source of intense, heated debate among God's people, and the world continues to escalate its godless, feminist philosophy, you will need to be well informed about this controversy. As a protector of God's people, keep up with the current debate on feminism (both secular and religious), biblical gender roles, homosexuality, and related issues. One way to be advised of current thought regarding these issues is to subscribe to CBMW News[5] (Council on Biblical Manhood and Womanhood). Elders cannot watch over the souls of the Lord's people today and remain uninformed about these matters. Our families and churches are at stake. Our young people need teaching and guidance regarding God's design for gender and sexuality. Those who are uncertain about the Scripture's answers to these questions are nearsighted, crippled shepherds who will be unable to protect God's flock.

10.   Why do we insist that Jesus Christ had to be born male?

   a.

   b.

11.   What does this statement from *Biblical Eldership* mean: "If Jesus is the supreme egalitarian that some would like Him to be, He surely failed women at a crucial moment"?

12.   Which sentences or clauses in Paul's epistles demonstrate that his teaching on male leadership in the church is universally binding on local churches today and is not a culturally conditioned instruction?

   a.

    b.

    c.

    d.

13. Western, twentieth-century people despise the words *submission* and *subordination*. Explain the biblical, positive concept of submission in the home and church (pp. 300, 301).

14. In *Biblical Eldership,* the following statement pertaining to the erroneous interpretation of the phrase, "there is neither male nor female" (Gal. 3:28), is made: "Following the same methodology of interpretation as the [so-called] biblical feminists, so-called Christian homosexuals claim the right to same-sex relationships." What is that methodology?

15. According to *Biblical Eldership,* what is the advantage to the local church of an all-male eldership?

    a.

b.

We close this examination of God's standards for biblical eldership with a call for you and your mentor to join us in praying great King Solomon's prayer for a wise and discerning heart:

"Now O Lord my God, You have made Your servant king in place of my father David, yet I am but a little child; I do not know how to go out or come in. Your servant is in the midst of Your people which You have chosen, a great people who cannot be numbered or counted for multitude. So give Your servant an understanding heart to judge Your people to discern between good and evil. For who is able to judge this great people of Yours?"   1 Kings 3:7-9

SCRIPTURE MEMORY ASSIGNMENT:

"Obey your leaders and submit to them, for they keep watch over your souls as those who will give an account. Let them do this with joy and not with grief, for this would be unprofitable for you."
                                                                                    Hebrews 13:17

---

[1] Stephen B. Clark, *Man and Woman in Christ: An Examination of the Roles of Men and Women in Light of Scripture and the Social Sciences* (Ann Arbor: Servant, 1980), p. 124.
[2] Derek J. Tidball, *Skillful Shepherds: An Introduction to Pastoral Theology* (Grand Rapids: Zondervan, 1986), p. 188.
[3] J. I. Packer, *Freedom and Authority* (Oakland: International Council on Biblical Inerrancy, 1981), p. 7.
[4] Clark, *Man and Woman in Christ*, pp. 334, 335.
[5] Council on Biblical Manhood and Womanhood, P. O. Box 317, Wheaton, IL 60189

SCRIPTURE INDEX

GENERAL INDEX

FUTURE ASSIGNMENTS AND DISCUSSIONS

PAGE REFERENCE IN STUDY GUIDE	ITEM	PROPOSED COMPLETION DATE

It is not enough merely to have an eldership; the eldership must be actively functioning, competent, and spiritually alive.

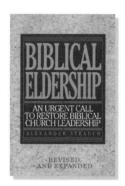

Biblical Eldership (full-text version)

This subject is vitally important to the local church, but unfortunately, it is often neglected or misunderstood. The result is that persistent, crippling misconceptions hinder churches from practicing authentic biblical eldership. Aimed primarily at churches or individuals seeking a clear understanding of the character and mandate of biblical eldership, this book defines it as accurately as possible from Scripture.

The Study Guide to Biblical Eldership

This tool for training prospective new elders or retraining existing elders consists of twelve lessons based on the revised and expanded *Biblical Eldership* (above) and includes many supplemental materials and practical assignments. The *Study Guide* is designed to be used by the prospective new elder (the mentoree or trainee) under the direction of a mentoring elder.

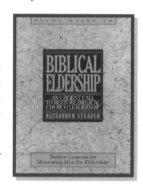

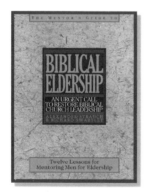

The Mentor's Guide to Biblical Eldership

This is a leader's guide to the *Study Guide* (above). It is an aid to the mentoring elder who may not have the time or adequate resources to prepare for mentoring. It provides extensive answers to all the questions in the *Study Guide* and offers suggestions on how to best utilize the questions and assignments. Highlighting aspects that need emphasis or clarification, it also provides helpful exposition on select Scripture passages and quotations from other sources.

Biblical Eldership (booklet)

This concise, 46-page abridged version puts the doctrine of biblical eldership within reach of every member of your church body and beyond. It is an excellent tool to use to teach a congregation about eldership or to raise men's interest in eldership.

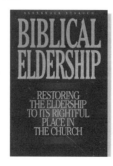

ADDITIONAL MUST-READ RESOURCES

Agape Leadership

This inspiring biography contains lessons on leadership from the life of R. C. Chapman, a widely respected Christian leader in England during the late 1800s. He was a spiritual mentor to George Müller and a friend of both Hudson Taylor and Charles Haddon Spurgeon. Spurgeon said of Chapman, "He was the saintliest man I ever knew." This book promises to be one of the most spiritually encouraging books you have ever read. It is recommended for all Christians in positions of leadership.

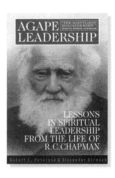

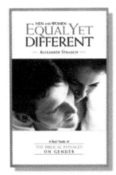

Men and Women: Equal Yet Different

Among Bible-believing Christians, intense emotional debate exists over what the Bible says about the roles of men and women. This book provides a much-needed introduction to the key terms, arguments, Scripture passages, and new research related to the complementarian (non-feminist) position on gender. It also presents the biblical evidence that men and women are created equal, yet have been given different gender-specific roles to fulfill in the family and in the church.

"Alexander Strauch has courageously not caved in to the pressures from contemporary culture or misguided evangelicals to become a 'gender blender...'"
—*John MacArthur Jr.*
Pastor-Teacher, President, The Master's College

"... *Men and Women: Equal Yet Different* lets the Bible speak for itself in the clearest of terms." —*R. Kent Hughes*
Pastor, College Church, Wheaton, Ill.

"[This] volume is strategically important. [It] gives an introduction to the subject that offers clear and easily understood information for the lay person as well as challenging considerations for the scholar." —*Dorothy Kelley Patterson*
Assistant Professor of Women's Studies, Southeastern Baptist Theological Seminary

"This book is one of the best investments of time and money on one of the most important issues of our day—and of any time. Take, read, feed your minds, clear your heads, and rejoice in and live out God's truth."
—*Dr. George W. Knight III*
Former New Testament Professor at Knox Theological Seminary and author of
"The Pastoral Epistles" in The New International Greek Commentary

"[A] welcome study of the important subject of gender roles. It is biblically sound and clearly written. It should be read by everyone who is seriously concerned about the future of the church." —*Jack Cottrell, Ph.D.*
Professor of Theology, Cincinnati Bible College and Seminary

A GUIDE TO MORE EFFECTIVE ELDERS' MEETINGS

Meetings That Work:
A Guide to Effective Elders' Meetings

Are your elders' meetings satisfying and productive, or do they drag on with little accomplished? Does your group spend too much time on trivial matters? Do you find it hard to stay on track when discussing important issues?

If you are less than satisfied with the quality of your meetings, you are not alone. These are just a few of the common complaints. The fact is, good meetings don't just happen. People have to learn how to lead and how to participate in meetings effectively.

This book is designed to help you do just that. It describes, step by step, how to implement changes that can significantly improve your elders' meetings. It provides insightful information that every participant needs to know.

Although it is written primarily for church elders, *Meetings That Work* can be readily adapted by deacons or any church committee to improve the quality of their meetings.

Part 1 gives a fresh perspective on the significance of elders meetings. Part 2, the heart of the book, explains specifically how to go about improving your meetings. It covers biblical ground rules of conduct, personal participation, communication tools, facilitation, and the specifics of good meeting management. Part 3 includes questions and assignments that will help your group evaluate its strengths and weaknesses and identify areas for improvement. It outlines a step-by-step plan for discussing and implementing the suggestions in this book.